THE LABOUR AND THE ROYAL

This is Éamonn _____ ok about
life in Dublin in the _____ gency years
t____ ___ ___ ___ies.

The story – and the memories – of the 'working lad' who
began his career delivering laundry, later became a
messenger boy in an elegant Grafton street shop, went on
'the labour', and later ended up with a desk job.

Delivery boys turning up at Switzers had to supply certificates,
a priest's reference, a bicycle in good condition and
a £50 bond – signed and guaranteed.
'You were lucky to get a job as a messenger boy even with your
own machine. . . the streets were full of rattling public cars, the
pubs full of rugged conversation; whole lives were spent with
the ration book, black porter and long working hours with little
or nothing in the pay packet.' *Evening Press*

Éamonn MacThomáis knows his Dublin intimately – he
learned it on his messenger boy's bike. He has an eye for
detail and a sharp and lively memory. 'Summon the local
historian in him and the man takes off,'
said Tom McIntyre of MacThomáis.

'**The book, full of humour, reveals the grim life
that so many had to suffer in those days . . . makes
one want to laugh and cry at the same time.**'
HIBERNIA

First published 1979
First paperback edition 1983
Reprinted 1985
The O'Brien Press Ltd.
20 Victoria Road, Rathgar, Dublin 6.

10 9 8 7 6 5 4 3

ISBN 0-86278-047-0

Typesetting Redsetter Ltd.
Printing Irish Elsevier, Shannon.

Sonas Mór ort, a Liam.

THE LABOUR
AND
THE ROYAL

Éamonn MacThomáis

Éamonn MacThomáis

Éamonn
MacThomáis

Illustrated by
Desmond McCarthy

PB

THE O'BRIEN PRESS
DUBLIN

Contents

For Rosaleen, my wife

Other books
by Éamonn MacThomáis

The Lady at the Gate
Down Dublin Streets 1916
Me Jewel and Darlin' Dublin
Gur Cake and Coal Blocks
Janey Mack, Me Shirt is Black

1

The Magic
of Castletown

ON MY FIRST WEDNESDAY evening with the White Heather Laundry I noticed the two stone figures guarding the entrance gate of the big house at the end of the main street of Celbridge. What sort of figures were they? Were they men or animals? They looked strange to me that day, somewhat like the strange horse with the spike in his head which guarded the gateway of White's at Island Bridge. At that time I had never heard of unicorns and sphinxes.

The two stone figures sat facing each other across the entrance as we drove in with the laundry van. We stopped just inside the gates and delivered a parcel to the gate lodge — opposite stood the church and graveyard, and all that I could see from the van was one lonely grave marked by a high stone. The avenue up to the big house was lined with lime trees, at least that's what the gate lodge man, Mr. Pursur, called them — limes and sphinxes — in answer to my questions. I decided the next time I'd ask him about the church and the lonely grave.

As we reached the top of the avenue and turned left, the big house caught my breath. I had never seen anything like it in my life. The magical house was sitting like a stone king between two great stone wings and fourteen stone pillars. There were several stone steps up to the dark brown hall door, in the centre of twelve windows; thirteen windows across the house on the first floor, and again thirteen windows across the second floor; fourteen windows across the left and right wings.

"You need not count them," said George. "There's 366 windows, one for every day of the year and one for a leap year. The window that's barred up, that's where the devil appeared."

Castletown House was like a beautiful painting, you could look at it all day and never tire. It was by far the most magical place of all my laundry journeys. I would have given my right arm to be able to bring the laundry basket up to the hall door and have a peep inside. But, the laundry was always delivered to the side entrance next door to the saddle rooms where all the harness was kept. The kitchens and servants' quarters were vast, but we never got a cup of tea or a slice of bread. We had to carry the laundry baskets through the kitchen to what was called the linen room. I could never understand why Castletown sent their laundry to the White Heather when they had a small laundry themselves: large, wooden wash tubs; tall wooden clothes horses; iron mangles for wringing out blankets; and dozens of big irons, some with wooden and brass handles. All along one hall were large stone sinks, and hot and cold brass water taps, and several bars of red carbolic soap, and white Sunlight soap.

The kitchen itself was the biggest I was ever in; you could seat a hundred people in it. There was a long, round table and a few small rough wooden tables, but only about six chairs.

Every nook and corner of the kitchen was filled with brass pots and pans, and a large dresser contained hundreds of red and blue-coloured plates, cups, bowls and saucers. Three big, yellow-coloured ranges were singing with the sound of water boiling and food cooking. The kitchen in Castletown was a place where my mouth would run with water as I sniffed in the smells, like the Bisto Kids. Among all the sounds, the big clock in the corner could be heard ticking the time away. On the cold winter evenings the kitchen had a magic spell, as my eyes travelled all around its walls and contents. No matter what time we called, the laundry was never ready. There were only a few servants, two elderly women, three young girls and two men; I think one of the men was the butler. He was dressed in a black suit and white dickie bow. The other man looked like the gardener.

The young girls were only about my age and wore long skirts down to their boots. They giggled as they passed us by, or brought down another shirt or tablecloth to be put into the laundry basket. I never heard any of them speaking even to one another — just giggle, giggle, giggle, as they dropped the pieces of laundry at our feet, and hurried away out of the kitchen door. The Castletown House delivery always took about three quarters of an hour, and before we left the big house we always changed the candles in the side van lamps. I don't know why we did, as the new candles with their short wicks never gave the same light as the old half-burnt candles with the long wicks. Redser said that George was afraid the old candles might burn out and leave us in the pitch dark in Castletown.

George always pointed out the devil's window as we drove away from the house. Looking back over his shoulder and pointing with the whip he would say: "There y'are now, that's the window (the one barred up) where the devil appeared."

During spring and summer we laughed at George and the devil, but on the dark winter evenings we did not feel like laughing. Sometimes I gave a quick glimpse backwards at the big house, but most times I kept my eyes closed and hoped we would get to Celbridge town.

It was at times like this that the magic of Castletown vanished and the big house seemed deserted. I often wondered what it would have been like if every room was lit up, and the driveway also lit with gas lamps, and all the horses and carriages and the ladies and gentlemen coming to a party in Castletown. It had a Cinderella Ball setting and this is what I used to be thinking about as George was telling the story of the Devil to himself. Redser told me later that he used to be thinking of the big picture that he'd seen in the Tivo picture house. It was a good job it was dark and George couldn't see that we were not listening to his story about the Castletown Devil. Redser also said that Daisy the horse, whose ears were usually cocked when she heard George talking, always had her ears down when George told the Devil's story.

Twenty-five years later I read a notice in the daily papers which told that Castletown House was up for auction and that its contents could be viewed at certain times. I organised a day off work and got the bus to Castletown Gates. The many other viewers to the auction rushed up the stone steps into the large hallway. I climbed each step slowly, after having first scraped the mud off my shoes on the iron mud scraper at the first step.

There was nothing in the house as I had imagined it. I was surprised at the black and white tiles in the hallway which looked like a giant draught board. It was the staircase that caught my eye. I could imagine the ladies coming down with their long blue or green gowns sweeping each stair. Apart from that moment in dreamland the magic of Castletown was gone — the hustle and bustle, the titter and chatter of the viewers destroyed the romance as they moved from room to room. I heard the awfully grand accents: "Oh no dear, it's 1712, I think." "Have you seen the red drawing room?" "Do be a darling and come to the Print Room." "That's the Speaker Connolly, dear."

I stood looking at the portrait of Speaker Connolly, the man who built Castletown and started the first Buy Irish campaign — William Connolly who was elected speaker in the Irish House of Commons, in College Green, in 1715. He was born in Ballyshannon, Co. Donegal, in the year 1662. His father was a wealthy innkeeper. William became an attorney and made a fortune by dealing in forfeited estates — he later stood for Parliament and was elected. In 1709 he became the Lord and Master of the Revenue; by this time he was the richest man in Ireland. He married Katherine Conyngham, the daughter of an officer in King William's army and the Conynghams were also in the big league riches.

The building of Castletown House was started in 1722.

"I want everything Irish" said Connolly, "Irish marble, Irish silver, Irish timber, and Irish furniture — I want to build the largest Irish house in Ireland."

Isn't it strange that a man with such noble Irish sentiments got an Italian to design his house? A claim has been made for Alessandro Galilei by Georgian historians. Yet, Alessandro left Ireland in 1718, four years before Castletown was started. I think I'd rather give the credit to Edward Lovett Pearse and John Rothery. Pearse was the architect of the Parliament House in College Green, the foundation stone of which was laid by William Connolly in 1729. Rothery was a Kildare man, born and reared in Celbridge, and following in a long line of famous architects — so you have a pick of architect Alessandro Galilei, John Rothery or Edward Lovett Pearse.

William Connolly, who had no children, died on 30th October, 1729, at his town house in Capel Street. In his will he stated that anyone attending his funeral should wear white linen scarves to support the Irish linen industry; thousands of heads draped in white linen followed his coffin from Capel Street to Celbridge. His widow lived on in Castletown on her own for over twenty years. In the year 1740 she built the famous hunting landmark known as Connolly's Folly, or the obelisk (or "nob a list", in my laundry days). It is said she built it as Famine Relief and paid the workers a ha'penny a day. The Folly is at the rere of Castletown and Mrs. Connolly had a fine view of it from her bedroom window. One can well imagine the Folly all lit up at night with rush lamps and candles, and the midnight huntsmen and huntswomen drinking wine and claret, and resting while the fox hides.

Three years later Mrs. Connolly built the wonderful barn at Leixlip. The barn is cork-screw shaped and was used for storing the grain from the lands of Castletown. When Mrs. Connolly died on 1752, Castletown House was left to her nephew, William. Two years later William was dead, and his wife and children moved to their house in Staffordshire.

For four years the House remained empty and then young

12

Tom Connolly became of age and returned to Castletown. The old speaker's will had stated that the master of Castletown had to live in the House several months every year. Now Castletown was owned by a bachelor.

One day while out horse-riding he met a young girl of sweet fifteen. She was Louisa Lennox, the daughter of the Duke of Richmond, who was living with her sister Emily, the Countess of Kildare, at Carton, Maynooth. Emily, who later became Duchess of Leinster, was the mother of Lord Edward Fitzgerald. Louisa was his favourite aunt, who was the last to visit him as he was dying in Newgate Prison, 1798. It was also Louisa who brought Lord Edward's remains from Newgate Prison to St. Werburgh's vaults.

Soon after the meeting of Tom Connolly and Louisa Lennox they were married, and Castletown House entered its golden era — lavish parties, midnight hunts, with friends and strangers coming and going. One stranger came, however, and didn't want to go — Old Nick himself, Mister Devil, as when he used his royal title, "the Prince of Darkness".

It was at the midnight hunt that Mr. Thomas Connolly noticed the dark stranger on the coal black horse. The dark stranger was a brilliant horseman and it was he that night who caught the fox; Connolly invited him back to Castletown for a meal. As they entered the dining hall the dark stranger spent several minutes looking at himself in a gilt mirror. He then examined the fire place, took up the poker and poked the large roaring fire; he sat next to Connolly during the meal. Connolly, who dropped his napkin, bent down to pick it up off the floor. It was then he noticed that the dark stranger had taken off his hunting boots and that he had cloven hoofs. Connolly kept his cool, and ordered all the other guests and servants into the green drawing room. He then turned to the dark stranger and ordered him to leave his house at once. The dark stranger laughed and told Connolly that he intended to stay for several months. Connolly at once sent one of his servants to Christ Church Celbridge to ask the minister to come quickly to Castletown. The servant returned to say that the Minister

13

had gone to Dublin and would not be back for three days.

By now the dark stranger had turned himself into many forms of four-legged animals, and was running and howling all over the dining room. Connolly could not bear it any longer.

"Go at once,"he said to his servant, "to the Roman Catholic parish priest, Father Malachy, and tell him I need his help."

It was three in the morning as Father Malachy got out of bed and hurried with the servant to Castletown.

There was no need for Connolly to explain; the dark stranger mocked the priest as he entered the dining room. Father Malachy went to work on the dark stranger with holy water, crucifix and missal, but all to no avail, as the dark stranger mocked and howled. Father Malachy, whose hair turned grey during the ordeal, lost his temper and threw his missal at the devil. The devil ducked, and the missal hit the gilt mirror and cracked it down the centre.

"Be gone Satan," Father Malachy roared, as he held up the crucifix.

The doors were locked, the windows were locked; the only avenue of escape for the dark stranger was up the marble fireplace chimney. And up he went, cracking the marble and twisting the fireside furniture as he disappeared in a puff of green smoke. The servant who had been looking in the keyhole was so overjoyed that he ran around the house telling everyone what happened. Soon the story spread all over Celbridge, Kildare, Dublin, Ireland and England. Ballads and poems were written about Father Malachy and the Devil in Castletown.

Was it a yarn, or was it the truth? Well, you can judge for yourself: the gilt mirror and marble fireplace are both cracked to this day. The dark stranger's visit to Castletown took place in the year 1801; two years later Connolly and Father Malachy both died.

Twenty years following that the then parish priest of Celbridge told his curate that he wanted to get rid of the large painting in his study. The curate told him that he was

14

foolish to do so, that the painting was a work of art and it only needed cleaning. The curate said that he knew a man in Molesworth Street named John Gernon who cleaned oil paintings.

"Alright," said the parish priest, "tell Gernon to call and see me."

A week later Mr. Gernon arrived. He examined the painting and said that he'd have to take it in to his shop in Molesworth Street. When he unscrewed the painting from the wall, there was a brass plate on the back of it which stated that this painting was presented to Father Malachy, parish priest, by the Right Hon. Thomas Connolly, Castletown, for rendering a service which could never be repaid. The painting when cleaned was beautiful. It was a portrait of Saint Paul casting out evil spirits.

During the auction of the contents of Castletown, I watched as each room became bare and empty. On the day of the jumble auction I bought several items — a wooden shaving mug, cups, plates, bowls, and a twisted iron poker with the devil's head on it. Could it have been the poker in the dining room the night the dark stranger called?

Today the wooden mug is with a friend of mine in Ranelagh. The cups, plates and bowls are with friends in England and America. The iron poker is with me in Ballymun. The articles were bought as souvenirs and links with the magic of Castletown in my laundry days.

2

Collecting Dracula's Laundry

AS THE DAYS AND WEEKS flew by in the laundry I got used to the idea of early morning starts and late night finishes; we had neither dinner hour nor tea hour. We worked hail, rain and snow for two shillings and five pence a day. I hated bank holidays as they meant we were a day short in the week, and on the following Saturday we had to do Friday's work as well.

Every Monday was the dreary day — fifteen or sixteen hours of collecting dirty laundry or soiled linen, as the lady in Clontarf called it. In wintertime it was hell; in summertime it was heaven. The only joy in winter was watching the thousands of ducks, drakes and birds of every description and colour, coming in to Bull Island Clontarf to spend their winter days. I used to think that the birds must have come from Iceland or the North Pole, because there were few places left that were colder than Ciontarf in wintertime.

I was getting to know the route off by heart, and George the van man was pointing out the different houses and telling the story.

"The man in that house was burned to death; Lord Charlemont lived in that house; that's Clontarf Castle — it's nearly a thousand years old. There was a doctor drowned there crossing the sea on a horse, on his way to Sutton."

Clontarf in the early war days was a very lonely place; the nice houses and well kept gardens were my company as I walking around collecting the laundry, I often passed Kincora, Seapoint, Sea Park, Mount Prospect and Dollymount Avenue without meeting a single soul. The loneliness of the long-distance laundry boy was broken by the laundry boy's poems and prayers. W. B. Yeats was my pal in Dollymount Avenue, Clarence Mangan was my pal on Kincora Road. I often looked out to sea and saw the Vikings fleeing in their ships.

I had other friends on my journeys: Wordsworth, Thomas Davis and Joseph Mary Plunkett, whose poem *The Presence of God* took on a new meaning far different from the classroom in St. Michael's, Keogh Square.

"I see his blood upon the rose," as I looked for the red rose in all the pretty gardens.

"All pathways by his feet are worn"

"His strong heart stirs the ever beating sea."

When the red rose bloomed the seas were calm, but when the red rose could not be seen the heavy seas beat over the Bull Wall.

I knew the name of every road in Clontarf, and now between my poems I was studying the names on the house gates and pillar walls — Bayside, St. Ann's, Blackditch, Vernon, Silver Acre. At night time when I couldn't sleep I used to name the houses instead of counting sheep.

Tiny was still the senior boy on the laundry van, and he knew the place where we asked the lady to let us climb over her back garden wall to save us a long walk around the block. George the van man had a new idea for quick collection — Tiny and I were to walk with empty sacks to the far, out of the way, places and meet George again at various points. Sometimes Tiny and I went together but most times we went alone in different directions. Then came the day when Tiny handed in his notice and left the laundry for a better job; I was now the senior boy.

This meant sitting on the cushion on the outside of the van, and taking over the senior boy's tasks in matters relating to the cleaning of the harness, the grooming of the horse, the washing of the van and how to pick the lock on the oats bin.

Seven new boys got Tiny's job but none of them lasted a week; the last kid said it wasn't a boy they wanted, it was another horse. For a fair long time we had no second van boy. In order to make up for the loss George the van man came up with a new idea; it was outside Gilna's shop on Caledon Road that George's idea was put into practice. I was given a bunch of green laundry bills, two empty sacks, and instructions that the first full sack was to be left at Butler's shop on the East Wall Road. I was to move on with the second sack and meet George at Dracula's House in Marino.

George was fond of his odd joke and he always insisted that Dracula lived in No. 15, The Crescent, Marino. We hated horror films and din't know too much about Mister Dracula, except that we wouldn't like to meet him after dark. What George meant to say was that Bram Stoker, the author of Dracula once lived in The Crescent, Marino. Even on a bright summer's day the house gave me the creeps, and while waiting for George I kept my eye on the windows and door, in case Dracula might come out to have his shirt laundered — in which case I had made up my mind to leave the sack of laundry and run like hell.

Soon the clip clop of Daisy's hoofs broke the strange quietness of The Crescent. George himself collected Dracula's laundry and gave me another bunch of green bills and two more empty sacks, one to be left at Hollybrook Road and meet again at Furry Park. We had our lunch on the footpath of Dunluce Road — a billycan of tea, and ten cuts of bread and Maggie Ryan.

After lunch came another bunch of green bills. This went on all day, even down the haunted Clonliffe Road. I was always praying that we'd never get a customer in the middle of Clonliffe Road; we had four customers at the top and six customers at the bottom.

The ghost of Clonliffe is either Larry Clinch or Freddy Jones: Larry was a highway man who robbed right, left and centre; he was noted for burning the Belfast mail at Santry.

19

Freddy lived in Clonliffe House and he was nicknamed Buck Jones. Now if the ghost was Buck I'd never be afraid of it, because when I was a chisseler Buck Jones was my favourite cowboy hero on the pictures. Buck was "The Chap" who we used to roar and cheer for from our wooden seats in the Tivo picture house.

I think Larry Clinch was a little bit of a Robin Hood in his own way: "Rob the rich and feed the poor." It seems a bit of a row developed between Larry and Freddy. Be the hokey, didn't Larry and his men ride into Clonliffe House on the night of the 6th November, 1806. Freddy (or Buck), who knew he was coming, brought in the Tipperary Militia. A big shoot-out took place and several were killed on both sides. Larry escaped but was later captured and hanged. The bodies of Larry and his gang were left lying on Clonliffe Road to warn all other highway men.

Later they were buried at the end of Clonliffe Road, at Ballybough crossroads. Down the years many people have reported seeing a strange horseman riding up and down Clonliffe Road late at night. Is it Buck looking for Larry? Well there's one thing I'm sure of, I wasn't looking for the ghost of Clonliffe as I ran down the road with me eyes shut.

Clonliffe Road was a great place for praying. A Hail Mary prayer for me Ma was followed by a Hail Mary for me Da who was dead, and another Hail Mary for me Granny. I was never short of Hail Marys or relations and friends to share them with, and I was never short of time to say them. The poems and prayers and studies of house names kept my mind occupied as I enjoyed the wit of my many customers.

George said that everyone you meet will teach you something; he was right. Mrs. Weston taught me two new words, "soiled linen". It was on the maid's day off, and when Mrs. Weston opened the door I greeted her and asked, "Any dirty laundry Mrs. Weston?"

A few seconds passed before she answered me. Then she said, "It's not dirty laundry, it's soiled linen." I never could see the difference between soiled linen and dirty laundry. In fact whenever I used the term "soiled linen" the person at the doors said, "What? What did you say? You're the laundry boy, aren't you?"

On my tours with the green bills I often collected up to eight or nine pounds, which was a fortune in those days. The green laundry bills ranged in prices from sixpence-ha'penny for a white hard collar, starched, glazed and fully finished, to one shilling and ninepence for a pair of sheets and five bob for a pair of blankets. It was sixpence extra for coloured garments or tablecloths, and we had to warn the customers that the colours might run in the wash.

The vast majority of our customers were well-to-do, but we also had a fair number of tradesmen and railway men around Phibsboro and Great Western Square. The poorest customers were the little old ladies in the Damer House in Parnell Street. We also delivered to a poor old lady who lived on the top floor of a tenement house in Morgan Place. That lady's weekly bill was ninepence — her laundry parcel was always a small copy-book size flat parcel. Now it was easy to tell what was inside most of the laundry parcels by the shapes in which they were packed— a hard collar stood up in the brown bag with a new white stud at the front and back of the neck. A pair of sheets or a tablecloth and even shirts all had their own special fold, but the little old lady's parcel was a mystery — all the bill said was "two whites" — ninepence. So on my way up the stairs in Morgan Place I sneaked a look — two lovely white lace-bordered altar cloths. I never saw the old lady's face as she only opened the door a few inches to allow the flat parcel to slide in and her ninepence wrapped in the green bill to slide out. As I went down the stairs I could see the old lady dusting the large glass shades over her statues and fixing her fresh laundered altar cloths.

My heart nearly burst with joy when George told me that he was going to get me a cash bag for myself. Oh, I felt so important. I could see myself with my leather cash bag over my shoulder and hanging down at my left side. the well polished leather strap across the chest. Wait till I get home to tell the Ma. I'd even be able to tip it up and let the silver

21

spill out on the lid, whenever some customer wanted change of a ten shilling or pound note. I'd keep the pound notes and ten shilling notes in the little side pouch on the bag.

When George handed me the new cash bag I nearly dropped dead. It was the end of a bolster case, black and grey stripes, stitched up one side, with a little string that closed the bag when it was pulled.

"Good, hard wearing material," said George, "which will save the lining of your pockets."

The day after the new cash bag, a new boy started with George. He lived in Rialto and had roaring red hair, and he became known as Redser. He was a happy-go-lucky boy and full of wit; we had great gas together. Redser had a favourite saying:

"If I won the sweep, do you know what I'd do first with the money?"

"No Redser, what would you do?"

Redser would fold his arms and look as if he was thinking hard, and then he'd say:

"If I ever win the Sweep, the first thing I'll do with the money is paint James's Street Church in bright colours of yellow, white and cream. Them dark browns and greys that's on it now really puts years on me."

Recently I was in James's Street Church and, lo and behold, it was painted in lovely bright colours. I couldn't resist asking the priest: "Father, did Redser win the Sweep?"

Redser was no time at all in the job when he began to talk about organising a branch of the union. He even had all my overtime money made up, and also the back-money I was owed, and it came to over a hundred pounds. I didn't know how one went about joining a union, and I didn't care to ask George. But for £100 I'd have asked Dracula.

Redser said he'd talk it over with the girls in the sorting office. When George got me to take Redser along on the green bills and empty sack tours, Redser discussed the union in detail. "If we don't get the rise, the overtime and the back-money, we go on strike."

"D'ya know the fat gerrel in the sorting office?" he asked.

22

"Well, she told me that Louie Bennett, the woman in charge of their union, was looking for a fortnight's holiday — with pay — for laundry workers. Just imagine, fourteen days free of work, with pay."

"Yer codding me," I said. Holidays with pay seemed an impossible dream that Monday afternoon.

Three years later, in September 1945, Louie Bennett achieved the fortnight's holidays with pay for laundry workers after a fourteen week strike.

When George heard of union plans he told Redser and me that we'd be sacked. We both said we didn't care. When I asked Redser how many members we had in the union he said: "two, you and me — the rest are windy." So I never got the £100 back money or the boot money that Redser was going to claim for the long walks we had to do daily — nor did we ever join the union in the laundry.

George said that his union looked after us and that we were too young to join the union. A few weeks later we all got a five shilling rise out of the blue; it was back-dated six weeks and we all got thirty-bob extra with our wages, but there was no talk of overtime or boot money.

3

The Low Road
to Lucan

MONDAYS WERE THE TOUGH DAYS, Tuesdays weren't too bad, but the best day of the working week was Wednesday. The country road meant collections and deliveries at the same time — Dublin to Kildare by horse transport, and back again the same day. It was always a sixteen-hour journey, but the country roads even in winter were a pleasant change from the rows and rows of houses in suburban Dublin. Besides, I had more freedom for my poems, and the only ones who heard them on Wednesdays were the birds, bees and cows.

The singing of the birds along the Lucan Road gave a wonderful musical background to my poems and prayers. The customers on the route rarely changed, except when there was a new one, or when someone had left in a parcel of laundry at the office and requested it to be delivered by van. One frosty Wednesday morning a new customer appeared — it was a large parcel of heavy curtains. There were two address labels on it; one with the name and address — His Excellency Senõr Vincenzo Berardis, Royal Italian Minister, Luttrelstown, and the other label with the following instructions: "The rere of the house is on the Low Road to Lucan, about one mile past the Wren's Nest, Strawberry Beds." To me that morning this was all double-dutch.

"Sure there's only wan road to Lucan," I said, "and there's nothing low about it!"

Beyond old Tim Healy's place and Captain Harty's stables it's all uphill. George, despite all his road knowledge, was lost as well. Paddy Norton came to the rescue. Paddy was the spare van driver and he knew everywhere.

"George, not bein' a drinking man, or never doing the Bona Fide, wouldn't know a place like the Wren's Nest" Paddy said. "George," he said, "Do you know the high path outside The Tap Publichouse?"

"I do," said George.

"Well," said Paddy, "that's where Sergeant McGrath waits for the boys coming from the Wren's Nest. If they can step up on the path from the road he lets them go home, but if they stumble or fall it's a night in the police barracks."

"What's the Bona Fide, Paddy?" I asked.

"Shut up you!" said George, "and take Daisy over to Kavanagh's Forge, and tell him to put a few good frost nails in Daisy's hoofs."

Kavanagh's Forge in The Hollow, Dolphin's Barn, was smoking away when I came up the lane. It was seven-thirty and Mister Kavanagh said he was working since six. I watched him as he selected the frost nails and drove them home into the hoof.

"What's the Bona Fide, Mr. Kavanagh," I asked.

"Be gobs," said he, "you're very young to be doing the Bona Fide."

He never answered my question. All he said was, "It's too early in the morning, son, to be talking about drink."

When I got back to the laundry George said it was o.k., he knew where the Wren's Nest was on the Low Road to Lucan.

As we drove out the laundry gate, the eight o'clock hooter of Wills' cigarette factory was blowing hard. A group of blue-smocked girls burst into a race down the South Circular Road.

"Ten to one," said George, "the ginger one makes it first to the factory gate."

He held the horse at the turn onto the road and we watched the finish of the race, and George was right, the ginger-headed girl was first.

26

"It's a good job they ran," said Redser, "or the factory gate would have been locked and they'd have lost a day's pay."

George frowned at Redser and told him to shut up — Redser was out of favour with George. It was due to his behaviour the night before. Coming down Queen Street, Redser lit up a Woodbine cigarette and continued to smoke it despite George's protests. Oh, only new boys were scarce, Redser would have got the bullet. I admired Redser. I would never have had the courage to do a thing like that, and when Redser offered me the big butt, I refused to take it even though I was gumming for a smoke. Redser told George that the ginger-headed girl was his sister, but George ignored him, and the rest of the journey to Chapelizod was made in silence.

After we delivered and collected in Chapelizod, we set off on the Low Road to Lucan. At the foot of the Knockmaroon Hill, Daisy slipped and fell. George had himself braced in the van, with his foot hard against the front van board. Redser was holding on to the centre iron bar for dear life. I went over the front of the van and landed on Daisy's back. So much for the senior boy's position — the cushion and all came with me!

"Quick," shouted George, "sit on her head, Joxer."

Tiny had told me about sitting on the horse's head when she fell, so without thinking I slid off her back and sat on her head. George's face was as white as a sheet, Redser had his eyes shut, and there was I on me own, sitting on Daisy's head, looking down at her big, white teeth and the white of her eyes — which looked like two big duck eggs. The road which had been deserted when Daisy fell was now flooded with people who seemed to come from nowhere — a postman, a policeman, a baker, women, children, and a milkman, all looking in wonder at me sitting on Daisy's head. I felt a bit of a hero and I was hoping that my face wasn't as white as George's. Later, Redser told me that my face wasn't white, it was green.

The policeman gave the orders as he opened the bellyband.

27

The baker, milkman and George unyoked the harness and pushed back the van. Now I was on my own with Daisy. Two women scattered ashes and clay at Daisy's feet.

"Right," said the policeman, "when I say three, jump up son. One, two, three!"

I shot up like a flash of lightning. Daisy lay there on her own for a few seconds, and then all of a sudden she shot up on all fours and scattered everyone around. George, who was now over his shock, moved in and took Daisy's head. He examined her legs for cuts and found a slight one on the left leg. He covered this cut with a lump of black grease that he took from the hub cap of the van wheel.

The policeman said he didn't think the mare could take the load up the hill, and that if we were heading for Lucan it would be safer to take the high road.

"The bloody Low Road to Lucan," said George. "It seems higher to me than the high road." With that, he said, "I nearly forgot about Captain Harty's and the others. Joxer," he said, "yourself and Redser get the parcel down, find the Wren's Nest and meet me in Lucan at Sarsfield's Place."

We took down the heavy parcel, and what a weight it was. It was like a ton of bricks. Redser, who was bigger than me, said he'd carry it up the hill and then we would take chances with it along the low road to Lucan. We waited until George had re-yoked Daisy to the van and then we set off.

It was one of the funniest walks I ever made in my life. Redser sat down about seven times on Knockmaroon Hill and each time he impersonated me, George and the policeman when Daisy fell. He said I looked like a flea sitting on the back of an elephant while I was sitting on Daisy's head. We laughed, and struggled with the heavy parcel of curtains along the road that seemed that morning to have no end. It was bitter cold but the sweat rolled off us. Fair play to Redser, he carried the parcel most of the journey. After what seemed like weeks of walking, we found the Wren's Nest.

"Another mile," I said, "and we're at it."

"I hope," said Redser, "she doesn't give us another pair of these curtains, or it will be Sunday when we get to Sarsfield's

Place."

There was no name on the large iron gate, and all the pebble stones thrown at the gate lodge brought no one out. But a man passing by told us we were at the right house. The gates were locked with a big padlock and chain, and a sign said PRIVATE. The gates were painted jet black and were very high with iron railings on both sides.

It was a creepy looking place and we were unable to see up the driveway as it turned to the left a few yards inside. The driveway was covered with a forest of trees on both sides. Redser was all for climbing over the wall but I wasn't too sure. Maybe there's a big dog. The PRIVATE sign seemed very bold and very compelling.

"Holy mackerel," said Redser. "The horse falls, we're nearly kilt, we lug the bloody curtains for miles and miles, and you want to sit here and look at the gate!"

"It's true," I said, "I'm more scared here than I was sitting on Daisy's head."

"Scared, me sister," said Redser. "Come up here on the wall and hand me up the parcel."

"Hold on a minute," I said. "There must be another gate into it. Why would anyone lock the gate? I can't imagine the lady of the house carrying around the big key that opens that padlock every time she goes in and out."

Redser wouldn't listen. Within seconds he was inside with the parcel. I was still on the outside.

"Are yeh coming," said Redser, "or are you going to let me go up on me own?"

"Okay," I said, "here I come." Just as we were about to walk up the driveway a voice sounded behind us.

"And where do you think you're going? Come back here at once!" We got such a fright that we stood still. We were nearly afraid to turn around.

"Will we run for it?" asked Redser.

"I don't think so," I said. We both turned around and there was the voice standing outside the gate lodge door. I don't know how old he was but he looked like Rip Van Winkle.

29

He was wearing a vest with sleeves in it, brown trousers, braces, and was in his stocking feet. We nearly burst out laughing when he said "Why didn't you knock on my door?" He looked us up and down and then he examined the parcel. At first he was going to take the parcel from us, but when we asked for thirty-five shillings and ninepence he said we better go up to the house. As we moved away from him, he shouted after us that this was the rere of the house and that we should have gone in by the Clonsilla entrance. We ignored his voice and moved quickly up the driveway.

The lady who opened the door in the big house was delighted with the job the laundry had done on the curtains. She examined them in detail and ran her fingers over the flower pattern, tracing out all the colours, and said it was a miracle that the colours did not run. She paid us £2 and told us to keep the change, and of course she gave us another pair of heavy curtains. I blushed when Redser asked the lady if she would have a couple of empty sacks to put the curtains in. The lady only smiled and said to go around the side of the house — the gardener in the sheds may be able to help us. The gardener gave us two fine, big sacks into which we put the curtains, and with a sack each over our shoulders we made our way back to the road. The four shillings and threepence tip was one of the biggest tips we had ever received. "Two and three makes each," said Redser, dancing along the low road with the sack of curtains on his back.

We rested at the Anna Liffey Mills and watched the men working, loading heavy sacks onto a big steam car. After a few minutes we set off again and didn't meet a soul until we got to Hills Mills, where again we watched the men at work. We next spotted the bridge over the River Liffey and the old Lucan Picture House.

"If they were open now," said Redser, "I'd go in and see that picture "Angels with Dirty Faces" and leave the curtains at the box office."

"And what about George?" I said, "waiting for us up in Sarsfield's Place."

"Ah, hump George and hump Sarsfield too," he said.

"How about a few cakes and a couple of bottles of ginger beer?" I asked.

We both entered the small shop and with the two of us and the two sacks of curtains the shop was crowded.

"You wouldn't be able to swing a cat in here," I said, as we called for two bottles of ginger beer and four blowouts, two five-packets of Woodbine cigarettes and a few matches with each packet. The blowouts were fresh, with cream oozing out of them and as big as small turnovers.

When we got to Sarsfield's Place George was waiting.

"What kept yis?" he roared and then he spotted the remains of the blowouts on my lips. "Yis were in a shop dilly dallying, eating blowouts, where did you get the money for blowouts?" We were afraid to tell him about the big tip in case he might claim some of it. He then spotted the two sacks.

"And what's in them may I ask?" he roared.

"More curtains" I said.

"Throw them up here," he said, "and if yis are this long next week it will be curtains for the pair of yeh!"

As we drove up Lucan Hill George kept saying that it was a mystery to him what kept us so long.

"It's no mystery," I said. "It's a long bloody walk, lugging a sack of curtains on yer back."

"To me," said George, "it's a mystery."

I then began to think that the only mystery on the Low Road was the estate of Luttrellstown Castle. Who built it, who owned it, and where did all the land come from?

The family of Luttrell came from Irnham, Lincolnshire, and claimed that their ancestors fought with William the Conqueror. In the reign of King John (1207) Geoffrey Luttrell came to Ireland and received a grant of lands of Luttrellstown in the county of Dublin. For four hundred years the Luttrells maintained their castle and lands on the low road to Lucan. During those years land and property were added to their estate, and by the year 1650 they had acres of land in Swords, Donabate, and Luttells-

31

town.

Simon Luttrell was M.P. for County Dublin, and Governor of the town and garrison during King James II's residence in Ireland. Simon stood fast by King James and fought with Sarsfield in Ireland and France. Simon and Sarsfield were great comrades and were both killed side by side at the Battle of Landen, 1693. I wonder was Simon listening as Sarsfield, seeing the blood flowing from his body, said, "Oh, that this were for Ireland."

Simon's brother, Henry, who was now Master of Luttrellstown was also an officer of rank in King James's Army. At the Battle of Aughrim Henry changed sides and led his troops against the Irish. Because of this piece of treachery the Irish lost the battle. In 1702 King William appointed Henry a Major-General in the Dutch Army. At the death of King William, Henry returned home to Luttrellstown and resided there until he was assassinated in his sedan chair, in Stafford Street, Dublin, on 22nd October, 1717.

Henry left two sons — Richard, who died while travelling the world, and Simon, who now became Master of Luttrellstown. Simon was advanced to the peerage of Ireland in 1768 under the title Baron Irnham. Thirteen years later he was created Viscount Carhampton of Castlehaven in the County of Cork, and four years later on 23rd June 1785 he received his earldom, the Earl of Carhampton. Simon's daughter Anne married the Duke of Cumberland, the brother of King George III.

Simon died in 1787, and was succeeded by his eldest son, Henry Lawes Luttrell, 2nd Earl of Carhampton. This was the man who designed the 'pitch cap', the 'half-hangings', the 'floggings', the man who had the credit of sending 1300 people on board the war tenders, without charge or trial. When a Protestant Minister called to Luttrellstown to complain about the half-hangings in Dublin streets, he was told by Henry that if he didn't keep his mouth shut he would find himself on a war tender within four days.

The war tenders were the ships that came into Dublin Port to recruit seamen — when their efforts to recruit failed they sent their press gangs along the docks to hijack any able-bodied men.

Early in 1798 several attempts were made on Henry's life, but they all failed. One of the attempts was made by the labourer workers in Luttrellstown. Shortly after this Henry sold Luttrellstown Castle and lands to Mr. Luke White, a wealthy bookseller. Luke had amassed a fortune buying and selling rare books. The same Luttrell was so hated in Dublin that Luke changed the name of the castle to Woodlands.

Whenever I hear the name of Woodlands I always think of the story of Patrick Willis. Patrick was the son of a wealthy bookseller who lived on Ormond Quay. He was a bit of a man-about-town and instead of being in Trinity College studying, he was in every den in Dublin drinking. Patrick was missing for three weeks. The father decided to cut him out of his will and turn him out of his house on Ormond Quay. Patrick told the father that he had been drinking for two weeks, but that the third week was spent in Woodlands with Luke White. Patrick said he met Mr. White in St. Stephen's Green and Mr. White said, "You're breaking your father's heart. I think," said Mr. White, "you should spend a week with me at Woodlands, and in my peaceful residence you should reflect on your life and the trouble you are causing your father, my esteemed and highly valued friend."

When old man Willis heard this it was like sweet music to his ears.

"Did Mr. White say that about me?" he asked. Then the old man began to think that Luke might leave them a few bob in his will if he died. "Oh, he said, "my good friend Luke White. How kind, how thoughtful, and he did all that for me. I suppose," he said, "you had a lovely time at Woodlands?"

"I had father," said young Patrick, "and Mr. White showed me all his rare curios, and books and paintings."

"Oh," said the father, "I'd love to see them. All is forgiven, son, your home is here. I'll put you back in my will this minute and here's twenty pounds to buy yourself a new suit of clothes."

The next morning the old man decided to go to Woodlands and thank Mr. White. He ordered his carriage to be brought to the hall door. He picked out one of his rare books as a gift for Mr. White and set off for Woodlands.

After a pleasant journey he arrived at the hall door of Woodlands. He was admitted by the butler and waited in the study until Mr. White entered. The old man threw his arms around Mr. White and said: "Oh, Mr. White, my dear friend Luke, your kindness to my son, keeping him in this beautiful place, telling him the error of his ways!"

"My dear sir," interrupted Mr. White, "are you mad? I have not seen your son for over twelve months! The last time I saw him was when I called to your shop on Ormond Quay."

The old man nearly collapsed, and Mr. White had to help him to sit down. The old man was white with rage and then he broke down and cried bitterly, and after a spell broke into sardonic laughter. A plan was forming in his mind as he bid farewell to Mr. White and Woodlands.

The next day he called on Major Sirr at Dublin Castle and he told the Major that his son was a member of the United Irishmen, and that if he took his son into the torture chamber on the old Custom House Quay he would get a lot of information from him. The Major was very thankful and could well understand the sorrow it was for the father having to report such a matter, but then the father's loyalty to the King came first. Young Patrick was arrested and brought to the Custom House Quay torture yard which was opposite his own house on Ormond Quay. While Patrick was being flogged and half-hanged in the Custom House yard his father was watching it all from the top window of his house. Patrick, not being a member of the United Irishmen, had nothing to tell, so he was cursed by the Major's men as being an obdurate villain. Patrick told again of his visit to Woodlands and soon the Major was riding along the low road to Lucan. After a few embarrassing raids the Major released young Patrick, who set sail for America and never returned.

In summertime the low road to Lucan is one of the most beautiful roads in Dublin. The road sweeps up the Knockmaroon Hill and down by the Angler's Rest into the Liffey Valley. It's lined for miles with shady green and yellow-leafed tall trees arching the roadway, wild coloured flowers, some growing on wall tops, staggering high banks on one side and strawberry beds in full bloom. On the low or flat side are the calm Liffey's waters, broken now and then by the jumping salmon.

It was here in olden times that men dug for coal and this is given as one of the reasons for the high banks. The Anna Liffey Hills were one time known as the Devil's Hill. The Devil himself was supposed to have built it in one night — I'm glad I didn't know that story when myself and Redser made our journeys to the big house with the laundry parcels. As Redser said, the nicest thing on the road was the Mill. I think it was the sound of the Mill which broke the silence on the low road in wintertime.

4

The Night Daisy Got Sick

DAISY'S TROUBLE BEGAN ON a Wednesday morning outside The Dead Man's Pub on the Lucan Road. The lady in The Dead Man's gave us a bag of green apples, with the advice that we were not to eat them, but to take them home to our mothers and bake apple tarts. George the vanman insisted that the apples were for Daisy the horse. We didn't even smell them as we watched our future apple tarts go down Daisy's throat one after another. In a matter of minutes she polished off six big green cookers.

The Dead Man's sure looked dead in those days. There was always a smell of turf burning in it. It had two big barrels of porter at each end of the bar and only a few bottles of stout on the shelves. The stone floor was covered with sawdust and it had three spitoons. There was always someone sitting at the bar, but no one ever seemed to be behind the counter. The laundry parcel always went in and out of a side door at the end of the bar.

An old man who said he was born next door to The Dead Man's told me how it got its name. He said that his father told him that many men were killed on the Lucan Road and that their bodies were brought to the pub where the inquest was held, and so it became known as The Dead Man's Pub.

"And do you know how they were killed?" he said. "Well, I'll tell you. Coming from the markets in Dublin, the men would fall asleep on their horse carts, and some of them toppled over and were killed by the wheel of their own carts."

The Dead Man's was always one of the landmarks on the Wednesday's load. It was here that we had our first billycan of tea and ate half our lunch. George also moved the load in the van more to the front to give Daisy a better balance. As he was moving the baskets he said to me: "How many more weeks have you got with us?"

"Seven," I answered. "In seven weeks' time my two year contract will be up with the White Heather and I'll be sacked. No chance in renewing the contract?" I asked.

George got mad and said: "Don't ya know bloody well there's no chance."

He then told me that I was the best boy and that he'd miss me. I began to feel sad at the idea of leaving, and I would have burst into tears only George and Redser remained silent. It was only then that I realised how much I loved George and the laundry, and even the Dead Man's. I decided to enjoy my last seven weeks and look out for everything on the journeys, and try and get as many stories as possible for me Ma. I mustn't forget to tell her about the Dead Man's and how it got its name, and also about Daisy eating our cooking apples.

Looking out as I was and noticing everything, I spotted Daisy walking slower than usual. Later, when it rained, I thought I saw more steam rising off her back than any time before; also her coat hadn't got its black shine. She had jet black hair that shone like boot polish; but now it looked dull. Then it struck me that Daisy was sick. I told George, but he said it was my imagination.

"Maybe she got a cold," I said, "from the hair cut we gave her last week."

I'll never forget Daisy's haircut as long as I live: George standing like a barber with the silver hand-clipping machine cutting away at Daisy's coat, and me holding the long nose pole. (A long pole with a rope circle on the end of it.) The rope circle was put around Daisy's nose, and I was to twist

the rope if she moved. I can still hear the roars of George:
"Twist it, twist it, yeh yahoo". Oh, as true as God, it was
hurting me more than it was hurting Daisy. I could feel my
nose getting smaller with every twist.

* * *

Daisy still seemed sick to me and I knew she was walking
slower when I saw the work girls coming out of the mills in
Celbridge. We were more than an hour late with the load.
When Daisy refused to take the canal bridge at Hazelhatch
George knew she was sick. The men living in the cottages at
the canal bank came out, and pushed the van and Daisy up
over the steep canal bridge. It was lashing rain, and some of
the men had no coats or hats, but they didn't seem to mind.

This was one of the things I liked about Wednesday's
load to the country: the people were always friendly and
helpful. Every man, woman and child we met on the roads
greeted us, and spoke to us as if we were their friends. I
tried this friendly greeting stuff in Clontarf one time and the
people thought I was mad; some of them even ran away from
me. Wednesdays were a joy. I could knock on any cottage
door and get the billycan boiled. Often, the woman boiled a
few of her own eggs and gave them to us.

When we reached Peamount that night George sent me to
Mr. Clinton's house to tell him Daisy was sick. Mr. Clinton
came out and examined Daisy. He said she had the colic,
and then he asked had she eaten any scutch grass or any sloe
bushes.

"There's something very green down there," he said,
taking his hand out of Daisy's mouth. I knew it was The
Dead Man's apples, but I dared not say a word.

Mr. Clinton went off to get a bottle of dose and we
unyoked Daisy, took off the harness, and put her in the
stable which Mr. Clinton had lit up with a hurricane lamp.
In a few minutes Mr. Clinton came back with a large porter
bottle which he said contained the dose. As George was giving
the dose to Daisy she bit the neck of the bottle and the dose
spilled all over the stable floor. The panic and excitement,

39

for fear that Daisy would swallow the broken glass, nearly put eight hands in Daisy's mouth as we all grabbed at the broken bottle.

"It's all right," said Mr. Clinton, "I have it." He went off again and returned with another bottle of dose.

This time, with George and Mr. Clinton holding open Daisy's mouth, I had no trouble pouring in the dose. Seconds after the dose Daisy threw up her guts, and the six green cookers. She then lay down and closed her eyes. At first I thought she was dead, but then I saw her heart beating in the dimly lit stable.

"She'll sleep it off," said Mr. Clinton, "and she'll be as right as rain in the morning."

"What?" said George, "can she not take us home?"

"I'm afraid not," said Mr. Clinton. "She'll have to say here for the night." George then asked if he could phone the laundry.

When George went off with Mr. Clinton they took the hurricane lamp with them. We stood outside the stable door. It was pitch dark. Suddenly, two big searchlights went up into the sky. The two pillars of light came towards each other, crossed back and forth several times, and then the lights went out.

"The Army," said Redser, "looking for German planes."

On that dark wet and windy night the Baldonnel searchlights gave a comforting feeling — even if they were looking for aeroplanes that might bomb us. When the lights went out a very lonely feeling set in. A few minutes later the searchlights came on again and stayed on all night, crossing the sky. The searchlights helped to kill the time till Paddy Norton came with the spare motor van. Paddy was shouting about the notice that went up on the screen in the Tivo Picture House and how he missed the end of the picture over us. When he started to tell us about the picture, George said we were late enough. We had to transfer the load from the horse van to the motor van, and while doing this job Paddy whispered to me that he saw all the picture, and he let on he didn't see the notice telling him to contact the laundry.

"No wonder we were a few hours waiting on you," I said. "Paddy wanted to deliver the Baldonnel parcels."

He said the soldiers never went to bed and that we'd be sure of something to eat in the canteen. George said it was too late and that we'd head for the Laundry.

We didn't meet a soul on the journey back. George and Paddy were in front of the van, but we were up on the open back, trying to hide from the wind and rain under dirty laundry. Just as we were turning into the laundry Redser shouted at me to look at the Banshee. Sitting on one of the stone bollards at the entrance to the laundry was a lady with long grey hair down to her waist. If Redser had looked over to the other stone bollard he would have seen a second Banshee. I recognised the two figures: one was my Ma and the other was my Aunt, my mother's sister. The aunt always wore her long grey hair in a bun at the back of her neck, but going to bed she let it fall down to her waist. She must have been in bed, and got out to come down to the laundry with my Ma.

It was twenty minutes past two in the morning by Anderson's clock as I came out the Laundry gate. My Ma and aunt nearly smothered me with hugs and kisses, and the two of them cried all the way home. I told them about the Dead Man, the apples, Daisy getting sick, the dose, the searchlights and Paddy Norton in the Tivo Picture House, but they never spoke a word.

As we got to the gate of our house the hall door was open and my other aunt, my mother's other sister, was waiting for me. She too was crying, the fire was blazing and instead of a dinner I got rashers and eggs, fresh crusty bread and doughnuts.

The four of us sat around the table, me and my three mammies. The Aunt Mary said she was watching the jobs page in the *Evening Mail*. The aunt Sarah said she was watching the shop windows for "Boys Wanted" in town. My Ma said that the time had come to ask her brother John to see if he could get me a job in Switzers, Grafton Street.

The following morning at half past ten Paddy Norton,

George and I set out in the motor van for Peamount. Mr. Clinton was waiting for us and, like he said, Daisy was as right as rain. George took Daisy back to the Laundry while Paddy and I delivered the rest of the load. I got a great welcome in Baldonnel. The soldiers were worried about me and their clean shirts. We both got our breakfast and got a great cheer going out the gate. When we got back to the Laundry George was waiting with Thursday's load. There was no time lost that day, and we finished up in Queen Street that night at ten o'clock.

My three mammies waited until I finished my rabbit stew dinner to tell me the wonderful news. I was to give a week's notice to George. I was leaving the Laundry to start work in Switzers. The wages were better, the hours were shorter, and I'd be able to get home to my dinner at dinner hour. All happiness was in our house that night, and the idea of going to work in Switzers gave me a thrill, so that I forgot about George and the Laundry. I can still see George's face when I handed him my notice in writing. He just stood there looking at me until I walked away. I said goodbye to all the customers. Every laundry girl and woman kissed me and wished me luck. The van boys bunched in and bought me a chrome-plated cigarette case which looked like real silver; it also contained ten John Player's Navy Cut cigarettes.

George got me a reference from Mr. Paisley, the big boss, which would have got me into the Bank of Ireland. Instead of the usual sixpence (for being a good boy) that George gave me every Saturday, he gave me a ten shilling note and said he would keep in touch.

As I walked up the South Circular Road that last Saturday night I began to think about the Laundry. It was tough, it was terrible, and yet I had a love-hate relationship with it. I loved the Wednesday's load; if only we had a motor car all the time, or if only I could stay on and become vanman — yes, become a vanman with a van of my own. So now my ambition was to become a vanman, and one thing for sure if I ever became a vanman I'd be kind to my vanboys. My mind wandered back again to the Laundry, and the new job;

and it all seemed to have taken shape on the wet and windy
night that Daisy got sick.

5

A Three Year Contract

THE INTERVIEW IN the House of Switzer was brief. The Uncle John had it all set up, so the job was mine. I wasn't even asked a question, except, of course, the list of items I had to bring with me on the following Thursday, when I started work:

1. A Laundry reference.
2. A parish priest's reference.
3. A birth certificate.
4. My Primary Certificate.
5. A good-condition bicycle.
6. A £50 bond — signed and guaranteed.

I was also told at the interview that I'd work Thursday, Friday, Saturday and get no pay, as Thursday started Switzer's week, and my first week's wages would be paid on the following Friday week.

As I walked up Wicklow Street I began to study the list of requirements for the job. A laundry reference — well that was easy enough: Mr. Paisley of the White Heather, had given me a powerful reference that would have got me into the Bank of Ireland; at least that's what my Ma said. A parish priest's reference — well, it was bad enough going to the P.P. for confession. After all, he was in the dark, with a wire grill to prevent him from hitting you, but just imagine having to call up to his hall door and ask there face to face, with no dark or no grill. I wonder would they do without the priest's reference. Would Fr. Doyle recognise it was me that was cursing and playing pitch-and-toss on the banks of the Grand Canal, the evening he chased us with his blackthorn stick.

It's funny, Switzers being Protestants looking for a parish priest's reference. I wonder would a Proddy Minister's reference do instead. That's a nice Proddy Minister up in St. Jude's on the back road.

A birth certificate — I suppose I'll have to go to Rathmines Chapel for that. My Primary Cert — shag the Primary; well, you're not shaggin' it now. It's a good job Macker and Roney Boy, my two last teachers, made me sit twice for it.

A good condition bicycle — the Ma said Mr. McHugh Himself, down in Talbot Street, told her he'd give me a bike; no deposit and only a half-crown a week. (Switzers didn't supply bicycles to their messenger boys.) They paid three shillings bicycle money extra. Well, I'd have sixpence to spare out of the three bob bike money, after paying Mr. McHugh his half-dollar, and I'd save on bus fares as well.

Now where in the name of the Seven Churches was I going to find a person to sign and guarantee a fifty pound bond, in case I knocked anything off out of Switzers. What if I did get the bond signed for fifty quid and knocked off two hundred and fifty quid's worth? What if I knocked off a thousand quid, and they only left with a man to cough up fifty quid. Whoever thought up that bond idea was daft. I could fancy myself asking the man coming out of the Grand Central Hotel, the man with the bowler hat, brolly, pinstripe suit, shower of hail tie and black briefcase: "Mister, mister, would you sign me bond please for the fifty quid." And I could imagine him stopping and opening up his briefcase to take his gold fountain pen from under his half pound of Hafner's Sausages.

Later that evening, as I was sitting on Jenkins' window sill at the Kilmainham Crossroads waiting for my Ma coming from work, I began to think of the fifty pound bond. Maybe Mrs. Jenkins would sign the bond? But we didn't deal in

46

her shop; I only sat on her window sill, and she never told me to get down. Other shops wouldn't let you sit on their window sills; in fact, some of them had iron spikes to prevent anyone from sitting down.

I knew an old man who used to carry a piece of wood, and he'd jam down the wood on the spikes and he always said that it made a very comfortable seat. Now if we were getting tick in any shop maybe they would sign the bond. You know, they could put the bond on the slate and we could pay off the bond weekly. Two bob a week would be five pound a year. We'd have it paid in ten years. That seems a terrible long time — ten years. Will ya cop yerself on, the bloody job is only a three year contract, and where are yeh going with yer ten years!

The Ma was only bursting with joy when she heard all the news about the interview. As she glanced down the list of requirements she said a little prayer between each item: the Laundry reference ("Thanks be to God and Matt Talbot"); the Primary Cert. ("Our Lady of Good Counsel, bless us; I must light another lamp in John's Lane"); the bike ("Mr. McHugh, may the light of Heaven shine on him"). You'll have to go to Father Doyle. I heard he gives lovely references. I have the birth certificate. She never said a word about the bond. At first I thought she didn't see it and then I began to think, maybe she didn't want to see it.

"Oh, God is very good," she said. "That's my prayers answered." At this stage I took a plunge with the bond.

"What are we going to do about the bond?"

"Don't worry," she said, "Dan Byrne will sign the bond for me."

"Oh, no Mammy no, not Dan Byrne, anyone but Dan Byrne. I'd even ask yer man with the bowler that comes out of the Central Hotel — or Mrs. Jenkins. She must know me for years from sitting on her window sill. Please don't ask Dan Byrne."

The late Dan Byrne, Lord rest his soul, had a small huckster shop in Mark Street. He was an old friend of the family and he used to deliver our groceries in a small brown,

47

matchbox-type baby Austin. He delivered the goods on Tuesday and collected his few bob on Fridays. On the Friday trips he sold cigarettes, as well as collecting. Every Friday he gave me a life in his motor car. I sat in it while he called to his customers. I copped the smokes under the seat and I knocked off ten Sweet Afton. I was caught — ate, bet, and threw up again by the Ma, and I used to hide up the back passage when I'd see Dan Byrne coming.

When I told my Ma that it wasn't right to ask Dan Byrne, the man I'd robbed, to sign a bond against robbing, she said: "Ah, sure that was seven years ago when you were a wild young fella. Look at all the money you handled in the Laundry and never touched a penny. Dan Byrne won't let us down."

I'll never forget the night Dan signed the fifty pound bond. He then took a rubber stamp from his pocket, dipped it in a pad and stamped his name and address under his signature, which made the bond look very official and important. He put his hand on my shoulder and said it was a pleasure signing and that he had great faith in me. I made a vow that night that I would never let Dan Byrne down.

Well, I took up the courage and knocked on Fr. Doyle's door. The housekeeper brought me into the parlour and Fr. Doyle gave me a great welcome. He was a different man altogether — warm, friendly and full of laughter. Oh, he knew all about me and my Ma, the widow. I was wondering did he know about Dan Byrne's Sweet Afton or the pitch-and-toss. He didn't mention it. He said I was a fine boy, and that he was full sure I'd be a credit to the parish in Switzers. He sat down and wrote out the reference and wished me luck in the new job.

Mr. McHugh let me pick the bike — a brand new black Raleigh with a silver-tipped front mudguard, and a half-white back mudguard with a red reflector on it. The bike also had a bell and a pump, and Mr. McHugh threw in a black bicycle lamp free of charge, and a pair of bicycle clips. The first spin was heaven: up Talbot Street, across O'Connell Street and along the Quays to the John's Road, Kilmainham and

48

Goldenbridge. As I spinned along with the wind in my face I rang the bell now and again, even though there was no one on the roadway. I saw a fella getting a nasty toss on the train tracks beyond Guinness's jetty. So I began to think that I must watch out for the tram and train tracks, as well as horse's, steam cars and people. It's funny the way something new makes one more popular than before. The night I brought home the bike the gang were all around our gate, and my bike. The advice I got that night on bikes would fill a book. The one piece of advice that keeps ringing in my ears came from an old man passing:

"Lovely bike, son. Take care of it now and don't be doing Stanley Woods on it." Stanley Woods was our motor bike racing hero and we were always his best supporters at the Phoenix Park Races.

I was ready now, organised for the job, and I thought Thursday morning would never come. It came at last and I made my way down Kilmainham on the road to Switzers. It was a bit of a push up Mount Brown Hill, but I made it alright and I was just at the Union gate when I saw the strange procession.

Out of the big brown Union gate came several women and young girls — many in grey and black shawls, some pushing broken prams and go-cars, and others with bundles under their shawls. They walked in a single line and didn't seem to be talking to each other, but some of them were talking to themselves. It was a strange sight that morning, but other people passing by didn't seem to mind or notice. When I looked back, the Union gate was shut and the procession was still coming down by Pigtown. I suddenly felt sad and yet I didn't know why, so I kept peddling down James's Street. It was the sight of the procession that made me sad; but what was it for? Who were they? Where were they going? As all this was going through my mind I found myself passing Christ Church Cathedral, and within moments I was coming down Wicklow Street, and into Switzers.

The porters and messenger boys from the House of Switzer gave me a great cheer and a great welcome. I was introduced all round.

"This is the shop steward. You'll have to join the Union, Liberty Hall. Yer man sells the coupons. Ya know like, the leading article coupons in the *Evening Mail*. You could win a fiver ya know. Christie runs the Diddley Fund. Hey Christie, here's a new member for ya. The Diddley Fund's great at Christmas. Keep him away from Rise a Row and don't mind that fella's racing tips. The wan he gave me last week — they're still out lookin' for it with a lamp. Here's old Jem now. Hey Jem, meet the new boy. He wants to know is there any room for him in The Westland Row Burial and Loan Society."

Ol' Jem kept his head down and never said a word in reply. Then he looked at me and came over quickly to shake my hand and wish me well in the new job. Jem was an old friend of the family who knew me since I was a baby.

The minute hand on the big black and white clock in Wicklow Street was at ten minutes past eight. Suddenly the hand fell to eight-twenty.

"Come into work quick." said John O'Keeffe. "If the hand of that clock falls again it will be dinner hour! We all clocked in at eighteen minutes past eight.

The timekeeper gave me a short lecture on good time-keeping and told me that he had the right to search my pockets as I was leaving in the evening. The lads told me that it was the timekeeper who caught most of the people knocking off. All goods purchased by the staff had to be sent to the timekeeper's door for checking, and were handed out as the staff clocked out in the evenings.

The first job I had to do that morning was empty the waste paper baskets, sweep up part of the shop and help Harry to carry the large waste paper skip to the furnace. Harry was as deaf as a post and every time I said, "What?" he'd say, "I'm glad you understand." Unlike most deaf people Harry spoke softly, so I was beginning to wonder was deafness catching. After we dumped the rubbish I was taken to the dispatch office, and introduced to my boss, Amos Gibney.

50

He was a small happy-go-lucky man, with twinkling eyes and brown, horn-rimmed glasses which he wore up on his head, more than over his eyes. He was very efficient at his job and was the quickest and neatest writer I ever saw. His right-hand man was Peter Farrell, the motor van foreman who was grounded because of the War and petrol shortage. He was a great soul but a terrible worrier. He sucked Rennies tablets all day and did all Mr. Gibney's worrying as well as his own. Despite all his worrying and moaning, Peter was one of the most respected men in Switzers. He was like a father to me that morning. Across from the dispatch office was the packing office, where my uncle John worked as a glass and china packer. Today he's over fifty years packing at the same bench, and has had the record of never having anything returned chipped or broken.

Alongside him in my time worked Bob, who packed the hardware, and at the other side Miss Daly and Miss Fullerton, who packed the soft goods. Between the four of them every item sold in Switzers for delivery was checked and packed. As soon as the goods were packed they were put through a hatch into the dispatch office. Peter the foreman called out the names and places as Mr. Gibney entered them in a large ledger.

Mrs. Hayes,
   Waterville,
      Bray.
2 soft, 1 hat, 2 glass.
Handle with Care.

And so the litany went on, and the delivery bays began to fill up with parcels and boxes.

The delivery routes were all based on the old town system. The Pembroke delivery, the Rathmines and Rathgar delivery, the Kingstown delivery. My first pal among the messenger boys was a lad named McNally. Macker, as he was called, took me under his wing and told me all the tricks of the trade. How to lay out the waste paper baskets behind the counters: a good layout, he claimed, saved ten minutes' sweeping in the morning. It didn't matter where I laid the

51

baskets, the customers in Switzers seemed to prefer the floor for their receipts.

At ten o'clock that first morning Macker asked me had I any money.

"I have a tanner," I said.

"Good," said he, "that's all ya need for Dessie's Milk Bar. Come on, will ya."

We went out by Thompson's Clothing Factory into Clarendon Street and turned the corner into Coppinger's Row. The Johnston, Mooney & O'Brien horse van was delivering the cakes as we got to Dessie's door. Inside, the small shop was like a messenger boys' convention. The Row was swarming with messenger boys' bikes: Pim's boys, McCabe's Fish boys, Leverett & Fry's boys. There were introductions all round; Macker knew them all. Dessie, who was a nice, friendly chubby-faced man, was all of a flutter.

"Now lads, now lads, let the cakes in. If they don't get in they can't get out."

"Two chocolate slices, Dessie."

"A jam doughnut and three Eccles cakes."

Cream buns, rock buns, apple tarts and pints of milk were flashing in hands all around the small shop. Macker said the first delivery wasn't till eleven o'clock, so that we had nearly an hour to ourselves. The Laundry was never like this, so I enjoyed Dessie's Milk Bar every moment that morning. The crack was great; it was all about the War. Lord Haw-Haw, the Union, overtime, muck boots and rain-capes, and stories about wrap-ups and deliveries.

In the summertime, Dessie had a long wooden stool outside his shop so we sat in the sun, drinking milk and eating chocolate slices. Every morning a small man in a black bowler hat and black coat, down to his boots, passed by on his way to mass in Clarendon Street. He seemed a friendly man, who always raised his hat to us and said, "Good morning boys." "Good morning Mister" or "Good morning Sir," we replied. This went on for a while until one morning a messenger boy attacked us:

"What the hell are yis saying hello to that ol' fella for?

Do yis know who he is? He's bloody ol' Billy Cosgrave. Up Dev, up Dev," he kept shouting.

Then someone inside the shop began to sing:

We'll hang De Valera on a sour apple tree
We'll hang Sean Lemass to keep him company
We'll hang Billy Cosgrave just to make three
And we go marching forward.

All this had me very confused. I'd have to ask me Ma about Billy Cosgrave, and I didn't like that song about yer man De Valera hanging on a sour apple tree. After all, wasn't I called after him.

"Ah, let's talk about the Union and Lord Haw-Haw."

"Did yis get the raincoats yet? We made our demand for the muck boots and raincoats, and if they don't cough up on Friday no fish will be delivered."

"Holy mackerel, it's not half-ten already?"

"Has any of yis the loan of a pump?"

There was a scatter of bikes and boys as they ran down Coppinger's Row and jumped up on the saddles, like Buck Jones, the cowboy in the pictures.

When we got back to Switzers our deliveries were ready. I was on city specials. By the end of the first day I had delivered to Trinity College, the Clergymans Daughters School, Earlsfort Terrace, The Russell Hotel, Bloomfield, Donnybrook, and several houses in Merrion and Fitzwilliam Squares. The parcels were carried in a large canvas bag, something like a post office sack, which was tied around my neck and across my back as I cycled along.

It was a work of art to balance the bag and the bike. After a few tosses I got the knack of holding the bag with one hand and steering with the other. When I clocked out that evening the timekeeper looked me up and down, but he didn't search my pockets. I was disappointed, because my pockets were empty.

I cycled up to Kilmainham Cross to wait for my Ma. She was delighted to hear that the day went well and that I liked the job. I still continued to meet her each evening coming from work. and the day I asked her about Billy Cosgrave she filled up to cry. I became embarrassed and I didn't push the issue or ask for an explanation. I was growing up fast — I was nearly sixteen — and although my Ma and I were great pals I felt myself growing away from her.

The chats around the fire got shorter, as I always wanted to go out for a spin on the bike with the young fellas and young wans. Then came the day that I no longer waited at Kilmainham Cross.

On the journey into Switzers each morning I always came in contact with the strange procession from the Union gate. One morning as I was cycling to work it was lashing rain and, as I came up Mount Brown Hill, I pulled in to shelter in the doorway of a public house right opposite the Union gate. Within a second or two the gate opened and out again came the strange procession: women and girls in shawls, carrying parcels, and pushing broken prams and go-cars.

A young girl about my age with a pack under her arm came over to where I was standing. She looked me up and down a few times, and then she said: "Give us a cigarette."

I gave her a cigarette and, after she lit it up, she said again: "Give us a shilling." A shilling was a lot of money in those days and I told her I could not afford it, but I gave her tuppence.

"Who are those women," I asked, "and where are they going?"

"How the hell do I know where they's going?" says she. "I suppose some of them is going to the Lock Hospital at 11 o'clock; others is going down to the Hot Wall in Bridgefoot Street, but it's no use them going there. Sure the men do be there from early morning, and no woman or girl could stand with the men."

"Who are they?" I asked.

"Who are they?" she laughed. "Some of them is unmarried mothers and others is pros."

It suddenly dawned on me that the pack she had under her arm was a baby, and that she too was an unmarried mother — I did not even know that such a thing existed. I

54

was shocked.

"Why don't they stay in? Why are they coming out in the rain? Why don't they stay in and sit at the fire?" I asked.

"Sit at the fire?" says she, "What fire? You must be mad. You have to leave at eight o'clock in the morning and you have to be back in at ten o'clock at night, because if you're not, the gate will be closed. Sure, once I had to sleep over there on McCaffrey's field myself — the gate was locked when I arrived at ten past ten."

I did not go to work that day. I was furious. I knew the story from my mother of the South Dublin Union in Easter Week 1916, with Eamonn Ceannt and Cathal Brugha, and how a handful of men fought the British Army. Then I began to wonder, was this what they fought for? What was the Union, who owned the Union, who made the laws and where did it come from?

My schoolday memories came rushing back as I sat in the wooden hut in the People's Flower Gardens. It was still raining and in the mirror of the rain puddles I could see the blue pills, the dead nuns, the stiffs in the morgue and the Seven Chapels. I made a vow that day to learn all I could about the Union, with a view to ending this terrible system that put women and girls and babies out on the road into the spills of rain.

With the study of the South Dublin Union came a burning desire to know every detail and every piece of history about my native city, its people and its struggle for independence. A three year contract with the House of Switzer brought me in contact with the Workhouse of Dublin and started another contract — "The study of Dublin and its people" — which has lasted a lifetime.

6

Ciro Pearls and Fur Coats

LIFE WAS GOOD. I was floating on air. I loved the job in Switzers. The shop had all the glamour and excitement which made it for me the most interesting place in Dublin. Every morning the big black window shutters were taken down, and not only did Grafton and Wicklow Streets come alive, but the models in the windows looked alive as well.

As we marched in with our sweeping brushes and wicker waste paper baskets, the charladies marched out with their galvanised steel buckets and their woollen mop cloths. There were about six charladies — all elderly, respectable ladies. With the exception of the Fur Millinery and Ciro Pearls departments, which were covered by carpets, the rest of the shop floor and stairs was covered with a cream and rust-coloured rubber-type lino. When this was washed clean by the charladies it looked brand new. It gave a clean, refreshing atmosphere to the shop. In summer it gave a cool effect and in winter a warm effect. I often used to think that if I could ever get a spare piece of the rubber floor covering, I'd give it to old Damn-the-Weather to cover his room in the Iveagh Hostel. Poor ol' Damn-the-Weather always said, "Summer is too hot and winter is too cold."

As we marched out with our full wicker baskets the two doormen marched in. They wore chocolate brown uniforms with gold cuffs, and peaked caps trimmed with gold braid, canary-yellow gloves, and gold buttons down one side of the long uniform coat. They were two ex-Irish guards standing over six foot in height, one with a waxed and pointed moustache. Their main job was to man the doors, opening them and closing them as the customers entered and left. They gave military salutes to the more important customers and kept out the undesirables as well. At nine a.m. sharp they took up their positions and the House of Switzer was open for business.

Behind each counter stood the black-robed lady shop assistants, with black silk dresses, black cardigans, black stockings, black shoes. Some of the girls looked stunning in black, while others looked as if they were going to a funeral. Black was the funeral fashion in those days. (Dare anyone wear a blue or yellow coat to a funeral!) I remember hearing a woman say one time, "Will ya look at that hussy in her red coat, and her poor father only eight months dead!" But black was the drapery fashion as well. The buyers were allowed to wear their own clothes. The gentlemen assistants all wore dark-coloured suits, some with white shirts and shower of hail ties.

The policy of the shop was a simple one: 'The Customer is Always Right'. To keep the policy in effect five floor-walkers were employed. They dressed in morning suits, tails, dickie bow and grey striped trousers, and red carnations in their button-holes. They were called superintendents and one of the five was the Floor Manager. Their job was to walk around the shop asking, "Are you being served Madam," and clicking their fingers in the air for attention. They added an extra something to the shop. At times they could be very nice and at times they could be right snobs. As well as walking the shop floor they signed all petty-cash dockets, and worked together with the buyers and counter charge-hands for the smooth-running of the shop.

Each department had its own independent staff. The counters were all glass, with brass and silver bordering. Every sale was double-checked and receipted in triplicate. In the ordinary run-of-the-mill draperies they had money railways or suction tubes to take the cash to the cashiers, who sat up on the second or third floor offices. But in Switzers the cash office was beside the counters. The accounts office on the top floor in Switzers was called the counting house. There were several cash offices in the shop and the head cash office was on the ground floor, beside the furniture department.

The outstanding departments in my days were The Times Library, The Fur & Millinery Department, The Ciro Pearls and The Perfumery, where I fell in love with Elizabeth Arden and Eleanor Adair. The Times Library was on the top floor. The books were arranged on shelves all at shoulder level; there was no bending down or reaching up. The books were carried to the delivery office on bread boards. Every book I delivered looked brand new. The best readers in Dublin were Mrs. Erskine Childers, Bushy Park, and the Misses Jacobs of Foxrock. Mrs. Childers got six books every Friday morning and the Misses Jacobs got eight books every Saturday. While the Misses Jacobs went in for romance and murder, Mrs. Childers went in for travel and world affairs.

The Fur and Millinery Departments were like private drawing rooms in a big house — carpets, gilt-edged large mirrors, and chandeliers. Almost every ladies hat was a patent hat, meaning there was only one of its kind made. The conmen used to stand at the windows in Grafton Street and sketch out Switzers' patent hats. Ladies Day at the Royal Dublin Society Spring Show saw at least a half dozen of the same hat that day had been copied in Switzers. Many's the day I was put on guard duty to watch out for the conmen copy-cats. I never caught any and used to spend the time watching the commissionaire opening the doors of the horse cabs and pony-and-traps, and helping the ladies down the step and into the House of Switzer.

The Fur Department had its own cold storage area and a rack of fox furs that always looked as if they were waiting for the race to start. The Perfumery Department was at the front of the shop and was in my sweep-up area. The fragrance of expensive perfume, and the rainbow of colours of lipsticks, eye shadows, skin lotions, powders and bath salts, together with the two large portraits (Elizabeth Arden with her red hair and green dress, and Eleanor Adair with her blonde hair and yellow dress), had me nearly love-sick every morning. Almost every month the Perfumery Department had a demonstration of skin lotion or eye shadow, or lipstick. The day after the demonstration I would have to clean up the mess. I used to pity the fellas who had to kiss that new orange lipstick that was selling like hot cross buns on a Good Friday.

The Ciro Pearls Department had a mystery as well as a magic. It was a small department in the centre of the shop, with three lady assistants. They seemed to do nothing all day except put pearls on strings. They also did a repair service. "Oh dear, could you do something. They rolled all around the hunt ball. I really shouldn't have worn them. I did find them loose at the embassy party. Could you be a dear and have them delivered by Friday?"

I remember the magic of the pearls, sitting on their black and wine-coloured velvet boards, and then the mystery. What are Ciro Pearls? Are they the Real McCoy or are they an expensive imitation? Well, whatever they were they had a certain amount of importance when they were being delivered to the ladies in Killiney and Kingstown.

I could understand Switzers having a surgical nurse employed in their Corset Department, but I could not understand why they employed a doctor. Everyone called him "the Doctor". He went around in a white doctor's coat and carried a tray with little bottles of medicine, some marked 'Poison'. If any of the staff got sick or had an accident they were rushed to Mercer's Hospital. So, what was the doctor needed for? It was a long time before I found out that the doctor was the official rat-catcher in Switzers. He called himself a rodent expert. It seemed the rats used to do their shopping at night when the shutters were up.

"Come down quick to the basement, the water and the rats are flooding the place. Get yourself a pair of Dunlop wellington boots, and bucket and brush. The corridors leading to the basement are flooded with water." The water was only about six feet from the shop as we swept it

60

back and back, and filled our buckets to try and clear off the rushing water.

"Where's it coming from? Is there a pipe burst? Is it the shores, or is it from a river?"

"What river runs under Grafton Street and Clarendon Street?"

"It must be a branch of the Poddle."

"It's a long bloody way from the Coombe if it's the Poddle!"

Well, as we kept the water at bay and banged the tails off a few rats, we discovered what river the water comes from. The fellas who lived near the Coombe called the river a branch of the Pottle, but those who lived outside the Coombe called the same river the Poddle. Well, Pottle or Poddle, rain or showers, water sure flows under the House of Switzer. I understand that today an electric pump keeps the same water at bay, and this of course keeps the rats at bay as well. After the water sweep-up we were all allowed to keep the Dunlop boots, which were a god-send for the snow and slush in Dublin.

The grapevine in Switzers was one of the best in Dublin.

"Come up quick to the Gent's Outfitting, come quick now or yil miss them. It's Jack Doyle and Movita. I think he's buying a pair of plus-fours."

There was a mad stampede down the dispatch office stairs into the basement, keeping an eye out for the floor walkers as we made our way up to the first floor to see Jack Doyle and Movita. Suddenly they both appeared: Jack Doyle, film star, boxer, Corkman. The finest-looking man in Ireland; over six feet tall, broad shoulders, jet black wavy hair, light tan-coloured suit, gold rings on fingers, diamond tie-pin, gold watch and chain, and big thick cigar. Every girl old and young would be swooning. And Movita was small, very small, and beautiful — dressed all in white, with white veil on her black hair and dark flashing eyes. What a sight they both were, standing in the shop and Jack buying shirts and ties. They were both appearing in a show in the Theatre Royal. The name of the show was "Something in the Air". Whoever named that show could not have named it better. Wherever Jack Doyle and Movita were, there was always something in the air. The people lined Grafton Street that day as Jack and Movita walked to St. Stephen's Green. They stood for a few moments at the corner of Duke Street to listen to the lady and gent who played the harp and violin, and collected their money in a large sea shell.

The next grapevine was Rita Hayworth, who spent £4,000 on clothes every year, and then Maureen O'Sullivan, Tarzan's Jane, who didn't look the same with her clothes on, and Maureen O'Hara, with her long flaming red hair. There was never a dull moment in the House of Switzer. The only moan I ever heard was from a young shop assistant. He always complained about the policy, 'The Customer is Always Right'. "It's not fair," he used to say. He gave in his notice and left. About a year later a new policeman appeared on the Grafton Street beat. It was the same man. "This is a great job I have now," he said, "and what's more the customers are always wrong."

7

Colours of the War

BY THE YEAR 1942 the Emergency was in full swing. It was illegal to sell flour without a licence. As far as we knew there were no ships which were prepared to risk the mine-swept seas to bring us wheat. So the Government made an order that the millers were to get 100% flour from the wheat. The result was black or brown bread.

Bless them all, bless them all,
The long and the short and the tall
Bless De Valera and Sean McEntee
For giving us the black bread and half-ounce of tea
But we're saying goodbye to them all
As back to the barracks we crawl
If we don't get cocoa we're going to go loco
So cheer up, me lads, bless them all.

When we weren't singing about bread we were singing about ice cream in an operatic fashion – La Don e Mobile:

My name is Paddy O
I sell Ice Creamy O
Down at the G.P.O.
For fourpence a tubby O
Go an' tell your ol' wan O
To give you the guinno
And come back to Paddy O
For the ice creamy O

The colour and quality of bread varied from bakery to
bakery. At first we ate it with our eyes shut. It was a funny
sort of bread — it didn't go stale, it went green. But when it
became scarce and rationed it didn't get many chances of
turning green. People borrowed slices instead of loaves or
half loaves. And whenever a shop seemed to have a large
supply the news travelled like greased lightning.

"Missus, the Coombe Dairy have lovely bread. They're
givin' two loaves to everyone."

The scene was like the Gold Rush days that we saw at the
Tivo Picture House, only instead of shovels the people carried
pillow cases.

"Go wan, mister, give us four loaves. I've twelve childer."

"You only had ten yesterday."

"Well I adopted two last night, they're war babies."

"Babies don't eat bread!"

"Don't mind that ol' wan Mister G, she's only five childer
and she got two loaves in O'Leary's this morning. I know, I
got two before her."

"Well, if ya got two there what are yeh doing looking for
two here?"

"Ah, it's for Jemmy's lunch. He has to have a lunch every-
day, Mister G. Isn't he saving the harvest of turf for the
nation on the Featherbed Mountains?"

"And what about my man," said the other ol' wan, "who's
down every day at the Victory Plot in Islandbridge, growing
potatoes for De Valera? Didn't Mister De Valera say we
were to grow more and eat less and that potatoes will save
the nation? Di ya know yeh could grow potatoes in a bucket,
and I heard a man on the wireless say that a nanny goat was
ten times better than a cow!"

"Oh, I must tell Jack to sell our cows and buy nanny
goats," the other ol' wan answered, and as she was leaving the
shop with her two loaves she turned back and said, "Don't
put too much trust in the potatoes, Agnes. It was potatoes
that killed them in the Famine."

The war to my Dublin was ration books, scarce bread,
scarce Maggie Ryan, a half ounce of tea per person per week,

trying to drink Irel Coffee (that came out of a bottle like sauce), black-out material draped on every house window, black shutters on every shop, barrack variety, the roll of the drums, the L.S.F. (Local Security Force), midnight matinees, workers playtime on every Cossor, and Crossley Radio. The signposts were all taken up and every bridge on the canal, Liffey, Dodder and Tolka was supposed to be mined and ready to be blown up if an invasion came. Tara Street Fire Station was protected by sand bags. The local defence force held mock wars with the Army. The police, who lost the spike and chain off their helmets, were teaching the L.S.F. men to do point-duty at Henry Street corner. And what a sight that was, as the L.S.F. blue uniform − with green armbands − held up the traffic and got a standing ovation from a great crowd of onlookers.

Point-duty in Dublin was an art in itself, as every Dubliner was a jay-walker. But then hadn't we the finest point-duty man in the world − Barney Connaughton, who did point-duty on Capel Street Bridge. People stood and watched him all day. Rumour had it that the New York Police Force wanted Barney to do point-duty on Broadway, but that Barney wouldn't leave Capel Street Bridge. His white-gloved hands were the quickest I've ever seen and his fingers danced the Bolero, as the bikes, horse carts, motor vans and steam lorries poured up Capel Street.

The conversation of the day was a discussion on Mandrake in the *Evening Mail,* and Inspector Wade and his Assistant, Donovan, in the *Evening Herald.*

War or no war we all picked out the best mot who we thought should win the Dawn Beauty Contest. The prize was £50 and a screen test for the lucky girl. Maureen O'Hara won the 1937 contest, and went to Hollywood and became a star. We used to stand at the corner and as a pretty girl passed we'd cry out, "Did you enter the Dawn Beauty Contest, Miss?" As the girls blushed, giggled or frowned we knew they loved every moment of our remarks. There were more Dawn Beauties in Rowntree's Chocolate Factory and Polikoff's Clothing Factory than in the whole of Hollywood put together.

The German Embassy on the Northumberland Road, with its large red-and-black Swastika flag hanging across the walls from the windows, gave a very war-like and frightening effect as we pushed our messenger boy bikes up the silent road. With my Republican tradition I was pro-German, and wore a German Swastika and Eagle in my lapel, which my brother had made in the shed at the back of our house. He made hundreds of such badges. Other kids wore R.A.F. wings, badges or red, white and blue crowns. The comics were all full of English propaganda and Rocket Fist Rogan of the R.A.F. was shooting down hundreds of German planes every week. Although I wore the Swastika I still felt uneasy passing the Embassy building, with its giant flag.

A lot of the older lads from the neighbourhood had gone away to join the British Army and Navy. One such lad, who was a great friend of mine, I think used to court my sister. His name was Dessie Garry of Kickham Road, and he was drowned at sea in the early days of the War when his ship was sunk. His death had a great effect on me at the time and I stopped wearing the Swastika badge for a few weeks. This was the second time in my life that I experienced such a feeling. The first time was when Liam McGregor also off Kickham Road was killed in Spain, fighting for the Reds against Franco. Liam was a lovely man when I was a child. He was the sort of a man who always had a smile, a sweet, and a word for children. Although I was told that the Reds were against my religion I prayed and cried secretly for Liam McGregor. I did the same for Dessie Garry. I played with his brother, John, Jim and Liam Daly, Sammy Mack, Ronnie Duggan, John Murphy (whose brother also was fighting in Dunkirk with the British Army). Dinny Murphy was another kind man. I often went for his cigarettes down to Denton's shop at the end of Kickham Road. Dinny joined the British Army before the war, fought on through it, and came back home again to Dublin.

Apart from the radio war news, the Lord Haw-Haw broadcasts and B.B.C. reports we were kept up-to-date at the local picture house. The American 'March of Time' and the British 'Movietone News' gave us all the pictorial details of Dunkirk, the Battle of Britain, the Battle of the River Plate and the Big Three at Yalta, Stalin, Roosevelt and Churchill together. The war would soon end.

The hero of the whole war to me was Rommel, The Desert Fox. I could nearly write a book on the stories that were told of Rommel, around Inchicore and Kilmainham. One that I always remember was the time that Mussolini was going to make a presentation to Rommel. The award was an Italian Cross studded with diamonds and gems. Before the presentation Rommel said to Mussolini, "Tell me, Mussy, what's yer Navy doing now?" The Italians had one of the biggest navies in the world and it hadn't fired a shot. Mussy got so mad that he threw the diamond cross into the fire and called off the presentation.

It was around dinner hour on a weekday when the news came into Switzers that the War was over. Soon, more news came of a big fight at the gates of Trinity College. The Union Jack and the Hammer-and-Sickle were flying high over Trinity and someone said that the T.C.D. students had burned the green, white and orange tricolour. Feeling was running very high and stones kept crashing through Trinity's windows. The ribbon counter in Switzers was doing a roaring trade. One end of it was selling red, white and blue ribbon and the other end was selling green, white and orange ribbon. Colours of the match were only in the ha'penny place compared to the selling and wearing of the colours of the War. The row outside Trinity was getting tougher and bigger when someone arrived from Switzers to tell me that the Pembroke load was ready for delivery.

As I cycled around Fitzwilliam Square with my deliveries and told everyone that the War was over and there was a big fight at Trinity College. Even though Germany had lost the War and Rommel was dead I still wore my Swastika and Eagle Badge. Within a few months the soldiers and sailors, and people who worked in the English munitions factories, had come home with countless War souvenirs and

68

photographs — Nazi arm bands, helmets, water bottles, swords, daggers, and pictures of Hitler and Mussolini.

My brother, Gerard, was a very good amateur photographer and he used to develop and print his own and everyone else's pictures. With a trick piece of developing he used to be able to make a picture of anyone arresting Hitler. Half of Inchicore could claim that they were the man who arrested Hitler, and had a photo to prove it! There was a large number of photographs of Mussolini's death — with his body hanging upside-down. I couldn't understand why Italians killed him, and he head of the Italians. My knowledge of war matters was very limited.

When I saw the first photo of Belsen Camp I thought it was a fake, British propaganda, and made up the way my brother made up the Hitler photos. But the voice of Richard Dimbleby coming over the radio, direct from Belsen Camp, glued all ears to the set. When he finished talking we were all in tears. I went for a lone walk up to the Grotto in Inchicore to talk to God and Mary, and ask them what was it all about. War, the killing of soldiers, and air raids one expects — but what of the killing of old men and old women, young boys, girls, women, men, babies, and all dumped in a heap like the rubbish at the tip head? As I came out of the Grotto I took the Swastika and Eagle badge from my coat and I threw it down to the grey water rats in the Camac River. Then came the American atomic bomb in Japan and the frightful pictures on the 'March of Time' series.

Outside the picture house life went on — Save the German Children Campaign; Meet the Mystery Man in Talbot Street this week and ask him for a ten shilling note.

"Mister, Mister, are you the Mystery Man Mister?"

It wasn't for the want of asking, but we never met the Mystery Man. The David Allen advertising boards told us where to get a glass of milk, two poached eggs and a large slice of toast for fourpence-ha'penny. And there was the advertisement for a bar of Cadbury's Chocolate. The war was over. Everyone was coming to Dublin for a feed.

"Would yeh like to join a shoe club? The coupon doesn't

matter. I can give you Number Six for Dolcis or The Standard, or would yeh like yer photo took in Ross's Studios?"

"Twelve weeks at sevenpence-ha'penny a week."

"Six portraits or a large one?"

"I can give ya Number Three."

Frank Blowers and the Shadows, Jack Tunder's Broadcasting Band. Free Bike Park. Spots Galore, Admission one shilling before 9 p.m. Girls in pink, blue, green and yellow twin sets, fur boots, crocodile handbags and golden brown nylons, crocodile gloves, and red tartan skirts. Children with music cases, going to learn how to play the piano. Steel balls crashing down stone air raid shelters. Shovels filling open trenches in Patrick's Park. Old men and women drinking tea and eating white bread. No more shutters on the shop windows. Bright lights, fancy models, furs and fashions. Window shop in pleasure, for the colours of the War have faded.

8

Is Kingstown Gone Yet?

AFTER SIXTEEN MONTHS working in Switzers I was promoted on to the Kingstown van. This was regarded as the senior position, and to prove the importance of the Kingstown van I was paid five shillings extra a week, and a half-a-crown a day dinner money.

You could get a four course dinner in the Goodwill Restaurant in Pearse Street for one shilling and fourpence: soup, joint, mixed veg., sweet, tea and biscuits. I won't say that the soup was water or that you could read the paper through the meat. It was a fair meal, for one and four. Sure it's no wonder the poor Goodwill closed down. But we seldom went to the Goodwill. We lived off bottles of milk, doughnuts, chocolate slices and the bookies offices.

My van driver, Pat Kennedy, Lord rest him, was a fierce man for backing horses. He followed Lawson's stable and I often wondered why.

"Shag Lawson," he'd roar, "he couldn't train a chicken! I'm not backing Lawson anymore." And that always seemed to be the day that Lawson won. "Shag Lawson, why couldn't the frigger have done that on Monday." Shag and frig were Pat's two strongest words.

I was only a few weeks on the Kingstown van when I started to back horses. My first bob win double was placed in Kingstown, and of course I won three pounds. From then on I bought the *Irish Press* every morning, pulled out the racing page and threw the rest of the paper away. Sixpence each week was set aside for the racing handicap form. I studied horse racing and horses harder than I ever studied at school. In next to no time I was a bit of an authority on who sired who, its last time out and how it ran. I also knew the horse's brother, sister, aunt and uncle.

I backed horses on the flat and over the hurdles, from The Galway Plate to The Cheltenham Gold Cup, The Derby, The St. Leger and every other tuppence-ha'penny race as well. Slowly I became a fiercer man than Kennedy for backing horses. I rubbed shoulders daily with the old men and ladies who stuck pins in the racing page in bookies' offices from Ringsend to the town of Bray. I had many winners and millions of losers. I had Airbourne when he won at 50 to 1 in The Grand National. Then someone in Dublin started the rumour that Mutt and Jeff gave Airbourne the night before the race. Mutt and Jeff became the best racing tipsters in Dublin. The trouble was that if you studied Mutt and Jeff too long they nearly gave every horse in the race. But every good winner was related in some way back to Mutt and Jeff. Among their favourite wins were Lovely Cottage, The Bug and Wokey Hole. The hours I spent studying the racing handicap form, and Mutt and Jeff would have got me a diploma in Trinity College or Goff's Bloodstock Sales in Mount Street. Later I came to have great respect for the ol' wans who stuck the pins in the racing page with their eyes shut.

The Kingstown van was an education in itself. The War was still on, petrol supplies were cut, so the van ran on charcoal. Again, being in the Kingstown van I was supplied with two pairs of blue overalls or boiler suits; one pair for work on the charcoal fire and one pair for delivering the parcels. Well, talk about a chimney sweep, you should have seen me after cleaning out the charcoal fire and reloading it. The fire was hard to start, but once it got going it never went out. The only trouble was the fire tended to clinker, so I had to get out on the wing of the car and poke the clinker to get the van up Killiney Hill.

Some vans had large gas balloons on their roofs but our charcoal fire was fixed to the radiator at the side of the van. There were two large cylinders, one for charcoal, one for water, and we carried a spare sack of charcoal. Two fills would keep the van rolling for about six hours.

We dined every day with The Earl of Meath. (We drank our milk and ate our doughnuts in his driveway at Kilruddery, Bray.) The Earl was fascinated by the charcoal van. The way Pat, my vanman, spoke to the Earl yeh'd swear they went to school together.

The Kingstown van delivered from Booterstown to Dalkey, Killiney, Bray, Greystones and Delgany, and home by Carrickmines, Shankill, Foxrock and Windy Arbour. Our first stop was the home of the late Count John McCormack, one of the world's greatest tenors. When I told me Ma about the delivery to the Count she played all her Master's Voice records of John McCormack and Richard Tauber.

The Ma was all a-go about Kingstown: "The cheek of them calling it that and its name Dun Laoghaire." To everyone in Switzers it was Kingstown, and the name was printed in bold black letters on all the address labels. The 'phone in the dispatch office rang daily at 11 a.m. The awfully, awfully Rathgar accent would enquire: "Hello, hello. Is Kingstown gone yet? Oh, don't let Kingstown go. Send me down the Kingstown Boy." I doubt if many of the shop assistants knew my name but they all knew me as the Kingstown Boy. And being the Kingstown Boy they all greeted me with beams and smiles.

It wasn't all happy stories that the Kingstown van brought to me. No — there was Mrs. Ball's house in Booterstown, where she was murdered and her body thrown into the sea at Shankill. I'll never forget the winter's day that Kennedy drove the van down to the sea at Shankill to point out the spot where the body was thrown into the sea. The sea waves were dashing against the rocks in that lonely spot as I prayed for the soul of Mrs. Ball. "The body was never found" said Kennedy, and at that moment I half expected her body to be washed up before my eyes. Then there was the story of

74

Honour Bright, the girl who was murdered near Sandyford. And the memorial stones which told the sad tales of the sea wrecks and loss of life off the Kingstown coast.

The most exciting view in Kingstown was watching the life boats go out in stormy winter weather to rescue ships in grief. The real character of Kingstown was in the faces of the yellow oilskin-coated men who manned the life-boats. In summertime Kingstown nestled between the pleasant Monkstown and the beautiful Sandycove. The old Salthill Hotel, which is gone now, stood up on a hill in Monkstown like a giant sentry watching the seas and Kingstown coast road. The old mail boat, the Town Hall, the Yacht clubs, the Royal St. George, the Royal Irish, the National, Victoria's Wrought Iron Kiosk and George's Pillar of Stone, the driveway to the Royal Marine Hotel, the street and roads named Clarinda, Albert, Crosthwaite, Eden, Crofton, all gave it a royal air to mix with the wax moustaches, eye monocles, bowler hats, old school ties, and naval caps with gold braid anchors surmounted by a crown.

Those were the days when butlers opened the hall door of all the big houses. There was one house in Kingstown which had a printed sign:

HOUSE PRIVATE
TRADESMEN'S ENTRANCE
TO THE RERE
NO HAWKERS ALLOWED

I disobeyed this sign one day and knocked on the hall door. The butler answered the door, but before the good man could get over the shock of seeing me and my Switzer's hat box, the lady of the house was at his heels.

"How dare you," she roared. "Can you read?"

"Yes madam," I replied.

"Well, read that sign," she said.

"It says 'Tradesmen's Entrance', Madam, but I'm not a tradesman, I'm a messenger boy."

The next day the sign read 'Tradesmen and Messenger Boys' and I was on the green carpet in Switzers. I think the only reason I went to the hall door was to see the butler.

Every day the Kingstown van brought a new story — "That's Boss Croker's place, that's Joe McGrath's house" — and Kennedy the van man knew something about everybody. As we turned into Grafton Street each evening Kennedy bought the *Evening Mail* at the corner of Nassau Street. One evening he told me to put my hand in his pocket and take out the paper money. As I took out the contents of his pocket a large crucifix fell on the seat. He told me that he carried the crucifix to prevent sudden death.

About a month later, as I was doing my morning sweep-up, Billy Gray rushed up to me and said, "Your boss is dead — he was killed outright last night going home from work." My first reaction was to think about the crucifix, then I burst into tears. Later that morning the full story came in. Pat Kennedy was pushing his bike up the Vevay Road in Bray, when a red Reilly car driven at high speed hit him and dragged him 100 yards. The car did not stop. Kennedy was taken to Loughlinstown Hospital believed dead. We contacted the hospital; he was not dead but very badly injured and unconscious. He lay this way for several days and then started to come around. He lost his memory. He did not know us or the Kingstown van which he worked on for forty years. He never heard of Boss Croker, Honour Bright or Mrs. Ball. He lived for many years after but I don't think his memory ever fully came back. The hit-and-run driver was caught in Greystones; the car wasn't insured.

Peter Whelan and Tommy Griffin, both dead now, Lord rest them, were appointed Kingstown van drivers. They were two of the nicest men I ever worked with. Tommy was a real Dub who spent most of his spare time helping John's Lane Church. He was a powerful singer and a great wit, and whenever he was on the Kingstown van it was a rolling show-house with all the old Cockney songs 'My Old Man said Follow the Van', 'All me life I wanted to be a Barrow Boy', 'Waiting at the Church', 'Lily of Laguna', and every old music hall song that was ever written. I wasn't much of a singer but I loved all these old songs and my Ma could sing them like

76

the birds. My rendering to the rolling charcoal concert on the Kingstown Road was 'The Little Shirt me Mother made for Me', 'I do like to be beside the seaside' and 'All the nice girls love a sailor'.

Peter Whelan was a Sandymount man. He was one of the most respected men I've ever known. He was a gentleman to his fingertips. He was a story-teller rather than a singer. He loved Sandymount and could never understand W. B. Yeats leaving his Sandymount birthplace for Sligo. Peter was very kind to Kennedy and visited him twice a week. Peter had only one moan. He'd point out a certain man in Sandymount and he'd say, "Do you see him, well that's the bloody fella that sat on me straw hat in the Star of the Sea Church."

"When was that, Peter," I'd ask.

"About twenty-five years ago," said Peter, "but I've never forgotten him."

A few years later when Peter died and we were bringing his remains to the church, one of the men who came forward to put his shoulder under the coffin was yer man that sat on Peter's straw hat!

During my last days on the Kingstown van two vacancies arose in Switzers — one for an approbation clerk and one for a house porter. When I applied for the clerk's job, I was told by the senior manager that I was only a porter and couldn't be considered for a clerical position. When I applied for the porter's job I was told that I was too small to put up the shutters. Both jobs were filled by men who wore Boys' Brigade badges. I couldn't help thinking at the time that if I'd been a few inches taller, or maybe had a Boys' Brigade badge, I might still be putting up the shutters in the House of Switzer today.

9

The Labour and The Royal

WELL, DESPITE ALL THE LABOUR in the White Heather Laundry and the House of Switzer, and despite all the royal times I had learning the geography of Dublin — walking in the footprints of kings, queens, princesses, bishops, beggars and rebels — I was now out on me ear on the Labour. No more would I visit the royal and historic houses of Dublin even if I did have to go in by the tradesmen's entrance. As I said before, you would have to experience the feeling of the difference between collecting dirty shifts and shirts, and delivering Ciro Pearls and fur coats.

Me pals at the corner of Kickham Road gave me the drill about the Labour Exchange:

"It's Werburgh Street ya go ta. Isinit, isinit Werburgh Street he goes ta? Gardiner Street is for those who live on the north side. Yeh don't bring a dog or a bike. Dogs is not allowed, and they won't let yeh park yer bike against the Labour wall. If yeh leave a bike in the lane or out in the street it will be knocked off."

Be gobs, me pals were right. As I turned into Werburgh Street the first thing I saw was a fella trying to knock off a bike. The front wheel of the bike was chained to a lamp-post and the fella was working at the lock with a steel knitting needle. The next thing I saw was Dean Swift's head over the doorway of the house where he was born, in Hoey's Court. The smell of fish and chips coming from Leo

Burdock's chipper made my mouth water. Maybe I'll buy a
single on the way out. As I made my way up the lane to the
Labour Exchange I saw the notices that me pal had told me
about:
NO DOGS ALLOWED, PLEASE DO NOT PARK BICYCLES
AGAINST THE WALLS OF THE OFFICE BUILDING
and another sign which said:
ANY PERSON COMMITTING A NUISANCE
WILL BE PROSECUTED
The Labour Exchange Building looked to me that afternoon like a suburban dance hall with a clock in the window
to tell you the time as you entered. Inside, the building
was like a large shabby bank; it had grill windows and
counters, and badly painted woodwork. In the centre of the
floor there were a few radiators against which old men were
heating themselves. A large sign over the radiators told the
men how welcome they were to the heat.
NO LOITERING. CLAIMANTS MUST LEAVE THE EXCHANGE
WHEN NOT REQUIRED AT THEIR HATCHES.
The Labour was packed with men ranging in age from over
sixty to sixteen years. The atmosphere was hard to describe.
There was no laughing or joking, but there were plenty of
arguments over stamps, times, Assistance money and days.
To me that day it was a house of despair, where some men
had lost all hope of working again. I handed in my cards at
Hatch 37, the cards were noted and checked and I was told
to go to Hatch 33. Although the Labour was crowded there
was no one before me at Hatch 33. My cards were handed in
for a second time and they were noted and checked again,
and then I was told to take a seat. I looked around and saw
about sixty men sitting on the wooden seats.
"Ya have to take your turn here," said the little man at
the end of the bench.
I sat down and the bench seats reminded me of the
woodeners in the Tivo Cinema, only the Tivo woodeners
were more comfortable. In a way the Labour was like a
Picture House with no screen. After a half an hour waiting,
my mind began to wander back to all the good days in

Switzers and the Laundry, and how I'd rather be walking along the coast road in the rain with a laundry parcel than sitting here doing nothing at all. I felt lonely for the first time in my life. There would be no stories for Ma about the Labour. It was all too sad. I'd tell her about Dean Swift's head and the smell of the chipper, and yer man knocking off the bike. I'd say nothing about the old men heating themselves or the signs telling them to get out.

By now an hour had passed and I heard my name called. "Are you deaf or something?" a hatch clerk asked me. "I've been calling your name four times. Here's your cards. You sign on Hatch 15."

I joined the long queue for Hatch 15. I waited and waited and after a lifetime got to the Hatch window. A small stub of a pencil was tied to a long piece of twine and tied to the grill window. I signed my name again and was told that I'd have to sign Mondays, Wednesdays and Fridays at 2 p.m. each day. I'd get no Labour money next Friday as I had to give two weeks' back pay.

I came out of the Labour Exchange and Werburgh Street looked different. Dean Swift looked as if he had his eyes closed. The chipper too was closed and only the front wheel of the bike was chained to the lamp post. I said a prayer for Lord Edward Fitzgerald as I passed his tomb in Werburgh Street Church, and made my way down his street and Cork Hill to the old *Evening Mail* office. I studied the Situations Vacant page which was on display in the *Evening Mail* office windows —

WANTED
VAN DRIVER, BAR PERSONS,
MOTHER'S HELP, TWO PLUMBERS,
JUNIOR DISPATCH CLERK — GOOD AT SUMS —
KNOWLEDGE OF DUBLIN ESSENTIAL —
APPLY BOX 303.

The job was right up my street. I knew Dublin like the back of me hand. I jotted down the details and the box number and then I began to fear sums. 'Good at sums' — was I good at sums? I often saw the clerks in the counting

81

house of Switzers totting up the books and matching up the invoices with the goods inwards dockets. But would I be able to do that and all the other clerical work like dictating letters, filing correspondence and checking bank statements. No, I told myself I wasn't good at sums, but knowledge of Dublin was like a drink of water to me.

As I wandered on down Dame Street and out onto the Quays I stood to have a look at the second-hand book stall outside Webb's shop. At that time I was a devil for history books. As I began to browse along the books I came across a book on accountancy. It was on the sixpenny stall. I flicked through it and couldn't make head or tail or it; it was all double Dutch to me. Nevertheless I decided to buy it. In later years that little sixpenny second-hand book on accountancy was invaluable to me as I studied accountancy from A to Z. Leaving the book stall I decided to spend the rest of the day at the Theatre Royal in Hawkins Street. There, for a bob (twelve old pence) I'd get a royal entertainment of a full variety stage show — Tommy Dando at the organ for community singing, and a full-length feature film which we always called "the big picture".

The Royal was a house of joy and I always left it feeling good, with the words of Tommy Dando's signature tune ringing in my ears: "Keep your Sunny Side Up, Be like two fried eggs, stand up on your legs, keep your sunny side up" and Tommy disappearing down with his organ into the basement, his hand waving goodbye and his voice saying, "God bless, cheerio, God bless."

As soon as Tommy was out of sight the spotlight caught Jimmy Campbell's baton as the sound of his royal orchestra filled the theatre. Sudden darkness again, spotlights on: the drummer Joe Bonny played a drum solo, and what a sight and sound that was as Joe made the drums speak music. Nuala (Noel Purcell), Nedser (Eddie Byrne) and the baby (Mickser Reid) were the most loved family in Dublin. Then there was Alice Delgarno and Babs de Monte's Royalettes, with magnificent costumes and precision dancing which often stole the show.

82

If ever you had to queue for the Royal you were entertained by some of the best street musicians and singers in Dublin. The queen of the street singers was Mick McGilligan's daughter, Mary Anne. I don't know the lady's name, but that was her song — her one and only — and she was known to all Dublin as Mick McGilligan's daughter Mary Anne.

The running between the Royal queue, the Royal stage door and Mulligan's Publichouse was like a mini-Olympics. I often wondered did the ghost of James Joyce ever slip in the Royal stage door to catch an act or see the big picture, or gaze in wonder at the lovely Royalettes, who would take the sight out of yer eyeballs, or listen to the golden voices of Sean Mooney, Frankie Blowers, Martin Crosbie and Edmund Browne's 'Down the Street Where You Live'. 'People stop and stare' — well they did in those days, stared at the wonder of it all — lights, music, singing, laughter, scenery — and stopped the shows many times with loud applause, feet stamping and whistling. From the last row of the gods on the upper, upper circle, down to the stalls at the colourful footlights, everyone in the Theatre Royal was united in one spirit: a deep appreciation of entertainment at its best. It's true what the song says 'There's no people like show people'.

One of the saddest sights I ever saw in Dublin was the day I watched the steel balls and bulldozers tear down the Theatre Royal for speculators to raise office blocks. No more would T. R. Royal present, no more would we see Pauline Delany in Hawkins Street, no more would we queue down by Mulligan's Pub for the old Royal. It had gone before and it was raised again, but this time it was gone for good. It was a mortal sin on Dublin and Dubliners to allow it to go. What would our fathers have thought of us who allowed a good, sound 1935 building to be torn down in 1962, when they moved heaven and earth to raise the Royal after fire had destroyed it on two occasions.

The first Theatre Royal opened its doors on Burgh Quay, where the *Irish Press* offices stand today. In November 1820 it was destroyed by fire. Within three months it was again ready to open its new doors to the Dublin public. The

THEATRE ROYAL, DUBLIN.

LAST NIGHT BUT ONE
Of Mr. KEAN Junior's Engagement.

Mr. KEAN, Junior,

(Of the Theatre Royal, Drury-lane,)

Is Engaged for a very limited number of Nights, and will make his Last Appearance, but One, This present THURSDAY, May 1st, 1828, when will be revived (never Acted in this Theatre,) the celebrated Tragedy of

THE

Distressed Mother.

Orestes, .. Mr. KEAN, Junior.

(His first appearance in that Character.)

Pyrrhus, ... Mr. CALCRAFT.

Pylades, ... Mr. MATHEWS.   Phœnix, ... Mr. CUNNINGHAM

Hermione, ... Miss LACY.

Andromache, ... Miss KENNETH.

Cephisa, ... Miss RAE.   Cleone, ... Mrs. MATHEWS.

The Performances will conclude with the Comic Opera of the

Lord of the Manor.

Sir John Contrast, . .. Mr. SHUTER.   Rashly, ... Mr. BROUGH.

Truemore, ... Mr. MELROSE,

In which character he will sing

A New Song, called " Oh! let me cheer thy aching heart,"

Above - The Theatre Royal opened in 1821   Top - Part of a poster dated 1828

An Address

On Opening the New Theatre Royal

19th January, 1821

Written by George Coleman, Esq.

and spoken by Mr. Farren

Hail, generous Natives of Green Erin's Isle;
Welcome, kind Patrons, to our new-rais'd Pile.
Three fleeting months have scarcely slipped away,
Since a mere waste this scene of action lay;
Not long the Block was laid, which all must own,
Damps eagerness, the slow Foundation Stone,
Ere expectation kept no more aloof,
The Architect was hope-crown'd with the Roof!
Brisk went the work—exertion still increasing—
Rods, trowels, hammers, chisels, never ceasing;
Labour was wing'd on Expectation's plan,
And every Labourer an Irishman.

At length, and following these wretched elves,
Behold another Race!—we mean ourselves,
Who leaning to our Predecessors' laws,
Now beg, most heartily, for your applause;
Beg you, brave Erin's sons, and Erin's Fair,
To make your Nation's Theatre your care.

Two wonder-working virtues 'tis confest—
Lurked in the Lamp Aladdin once possess'd;
Beyond all common method or device,
It raised both House and Money in a trice.
Our Building the first wonder keeps in view;
The second miracle remains with you.
Crowd hither nightly, then, from every quarter.
Till coin in speed has rivall'd Brick and Mortar.

(The above is a shortened version of the poem).

Dublin people performed the miracle and the Theatre Royal drew nightly crowds from every quarter. Eleven months short of its diamond jubilee the old Royal was again destroyed by fire. The event this time was more tragic than the fire of 1820 because its manager, Mr. Francis Egerton, lost his life. It was Monday, 10th February 1880. At 2 p.m. that day the curtain was to have been raised upon the pantomime of 'Ali Baba', the proceeds of which were for the Dublin Charities Fund, but at 12 noon the Theatre Royal was in rubble and dust. The newspapers of the time stated that "no disaster that had occurred before in Dublin caused such widespread feeling, and the sympathy extended by the people showed that the old Royal was part of the heart of every man, woman and child in Dublin."

Among all the stories of the burning of the old Royal handed down by the grannies and grandads there is special pride of place for the late Francis Egerton, who lost his life trying to save part of the scenery, or some of the costumes. Seventeen years later the Theatre Royal reopened.

'And brighter lives to come through many an unborn year'. Well, it brightened my life that day, after I left the Labour Exchange in Werburgh Street. During the interval when the safety curtain was down I composed in my mind my application for the 'Junior Dispatch Clerk'. I forgot about the part, 'good at sums', and let my mind ramble on, 'knowledge of Dublin essential'.

When the show was over I left the Theatre Royal, happy in my mind that knowledge of Dublin would stand me well if I got an interview for the job. After my tea, with a promise from Ma to light a lamp in John's Lane, I sat down and wrote out my application. I got up on my bike and went for a spin down to the *Evening Mail* office. The man behind the counter took my letter and put it into a pigeon-hole shelf. I noticed there were about six other letters in the same hole.

Two days later a letter came by evening post. My brother picked it up in the hall and held it to the light of the window. "It's for you," he shouted. "It's from a shipping company. Look, look," he said, "you can see the ship through the envelope." I must admit I was a bit at sea myself, trying to figure out the connection between ships and knowledge of Dublin — unless it was canal boats, and they wanted you to know all the canal locks. I opened the letter and it was from P. Donnelly & Sons Ltd., Coal Merchants, 37 Westmoreland Street, Dublin.

Dear Mr. Thomas,
  Please present yourself for interview at our George's Quay office at 11 a.m. sharp on Thursday next.

I could feel my heart beating. I was half-way there, the other half was the interview, sums and Dublin. The new job looked good. I read the interview letter more than fifty times and I began to get the feeling that my knowledge of Dublin would swing it.

10

A White Collar Jem Larkin

THE MA WAS DELIGHTED with the interview letter for the clerk's job. She kept asking now and again, "Give us another look at it." Then she'd hold her reading glasses over the letter and read it aloud slowly. The Aunt Mary who was putting up a new mantlepiece cloth turned around and said, "Ah, put that bloody letter away. I'm sick listening to it!"

I think she was afraid I'd fail the sums and wouldn't get the job, so she started to jeer the letter.

"Oh, a clerk. God bless the mark. A tuppence-ha'penny, white-collar clerk. I hope yeh won't be like the white-collar clerks in the Grand Canal company that loaded the canal barges when the workers were on strike for more pay." And then she quoted Jem Larkin. 'Beware of the white-collar, men. They'd load the coal and do the carters' work just to please the bosses.' A tuppence ha'penny clerk. God bless the mark."

As well as being Republicans our family were Larkinites. I knew the story backwards of the great lock-out of 1913, when the tram-men left the trams on the road during Horse Show week at Ballsbridge. My Ma used to sing and dance at the Liberty Hall concerts and was a great friend of Sean Connolly, who was killed in action at City Hall when he was attacking Dublin Castle during the 1916 Rising. Some children are brought up on cornflakes and porridge. I was brought up on Larkin and Easter Week.

I was worried and hurt by my aunt's remarks, but when she saw my sad eyes she burst out crying and hugged me. She was really afraid I'd fail at the sums and she was trying to soften the blow she thought was coming by running down the clerk's job. But the clerks doing the dockers' work was a pill she could never swallow. "Don't worry," I said, "I won't scab it on the dockers, nor will I ever be a black-leg." There and then I made a pledge to Jem Larkin that I'd never pass a strike picket as long as I lived, nor would I ever do a bad turn on the dockers.

On the Thursday interview morning I was up bright and early and looked like a new pin as I cycled in to George's Quay. It was twenty minutes to eleven by the Custom House clock, so I decided to spin down the Quays to kill a few more minutes and to walk in sharp at eleven for the interview. I soon spotted City Quay Church, so I went in and lit a penny candle to Our Lady and prayed that I'd get the job. The clock in Donnelly's coal office was striking eleven as Mr. Lyons came out to greet me. I liked him at first sight. He was young, yet bald, and had twinkling eyes that smiled as well as his lips. He brought me into an inner office and the interview began. There were no sums, thank God; the entire interview was spent with questions about Dublin. Name six streets that are near each other. Name six roads in Clontarf. Name four squares in Dublin." The answers came from the tips of my fingers and then he said he'd phone Mr. Amos Gibney of Switzers to get a verbal reference. He left me sitting alone in the room as he went to telephone.

I looked out the office window and really saw the Custom House for the first time. It was shining in the sun in all its glory. It seemed to be sitting and reflecting in the green Liffey waters. As my eyes travelled all over the Custom House I spotted the river masks, and decided that I would have a closer look after the interview. As I was still gazing at this wonder of Dublin Mr. Lyons returned. He told me that my reference was excellent and so was my knowledge of Dublin, and when could I start in the new job.

"As soon as you like," I said.

"Good." says he. "Tomorrow morning at 8 a.m., at Spencer Dock coalyard office. Ask for Mr. Colin Stokes — he'll be expecting you. Bring your cards with you tomorrow."

It was ten minutes to twelve by the Custom House clock, as I came out of Donnelly's office. The first thing I began to think about was my cards in the Labour Exchange. I decided, however, to have a close look at the Custom House and a spin down to Spencer Dock to know exactly where I was to go the following morning. As I crossed Butt Bridge I began to think of my pledge to Jem Larkin, and I let my eyes roll over the old Liberty Hall building which at one time was the Northumberland Hotel, and before that the Victoria Hotel.

I was full of the joy of the job: no more Labour Exchange but royal times again. The joy that was going to be in Ma's eyes when she heard about the interview and the Friday morning start. The wages were five shillings more than my leaving pay in Switzers.

But the magic of the morning were the river masks on the Custom House. I went from one to the other examining each mask in detail, but not knowing at the time that they represented the thirteen principal rivers in Ireland, and the Atlantic Ocean. Oh, if only I could draw or sketch these river masks for Ma! I was hopeless at drawing, so I made a few rough notes on the details of each mask: fishes in his beard, a scarf around his neck, cabbage in his head; an ugly man, and only one woman's head.

They say that James Gandon, who designed and built the Custom House, had a chief stone-cutter by the name of Darley. One day Darley said to Gandon, "Excuse me, Mr. Gandon, but would you have any carving work for a young fella in my stone yard named Eddie Smyth. He's a grand lad with a powerful pair of hands and he can carve anything in stone." So Gandon gave Edward Smyth the job and the river masks are the result of his work. That job was the start of a long relationship between Gandon and Smyth, and Smyth's son John continued in his father's footsteps as a sculptor.

I passed on from the Custom House that day to George's Dock, and down by the B & I sheds and the Liverpool Boat to Guild Street and Spencer Dock. I cycled on to Sheriff Street and went into St. Lawrence O'Toole's Church to thank God for the job and ask his help with the sums. When I entered the church, I knelt in Matt Talbot's favourite spot to thank him also for putting in a word about the job, and for helping Ma down the lean years. As I came out of the church I decided on one more call before I'd go to the Labour for my cards. The call was to Woolers, or Woolworths, Henry Street, to buy a few coloured markers. I didn't know what I was going to colour or what I was going to mark, but if I wasn't good at sums I was going to look good with four coloured markers sticking out of my top pocket. A red, a green, a blue, and a black made me a colourful-looking clerk as I walked into the Labour Exchange and requested my cards back.

Then the trouble started — they couldn't find my cards. After running around the hatches this man asked me how long I was on the labour.

"Since Monday," I said. He nearly died with fright.

"Monday," he roared. "Last Monday, only last Monday? Sure the ink isn't dry on them yet."

It seems the cards hadn't got to where they were supposed to go. They were in between hatches, and a terrible fuss was caused at taking them out at the half-way stage.

"This doesn't happen," said the man. "Are you sure it was only last Monday?" At this stage I was about to call in St. Anthony and Matt Talbot when the cards were found.

Walking out of the Labour Exchange I felt like a million dollars, and with a bit of luck and a bit of help with the sums I wouldn't be back. We had a little party that night, and the Ma and my aunts cried their eyes out. We had a great discussion on the river masks, my pledge to Larkin, the old Liberty Hall and Matt's church.

At seven a.m. the next morning I was on my way by bike to Spencer Dock. I flew down the John's Road, along the Quays and hit O'Connell Bridge at seven thirty, which meant

I'd about twenty minutes to spare to have another look at the river masks.

The first day in the office flew by. Mr. Colin Stokes, the office manager, introduced me to the staff and told me my job was to enter the delivery dockets in the large posting docket book. It all had to be a pen and ink entry. There were no cheap Biros in those days — so I had to use an N-type pen like my old school pens, and dip all day into the large steel inkwell. Towards evening I'd a welt on my finger from writing, which I still have to this day. The delivery dockets had about twenty words, and I often wrote over 600 in a day. As well as the name and address details there was a weight column — tons, cwts., qtrs., lbs. — and a money column — £ s. d. or pounds, shillings and pence.

As I flicked back the pages of the posting docket book on the first day, nearly every entry read £2.19.11. or £3.16.7. Half-way through the day I was told to check my tots and see if they agreed with the weighbridge ledger. I took the tots or the sums slowly, and prayed quickly. I double-checked and got the same answers. I'd go over it again before I'd call out my figures. I must have checked it six times, and the sweat was rolling off me as I called out the half-way total. I nearly fell off the chair when I was told that the tot was correct. There were no adding machines — every tot was worked out in the mind.

The day's work ended at six-thirty, and I called out the complete total. This time the answers came back fast.

"You're wrong, you're wrong. You're thirty-two tons too much!"

Well, I totted again and again, and still got the same answer. By now it was a quarter to eight and we were still wrong. The books must balance each day. Mr. Stokes was very nice about the whole affair, but the weigh clerk kept insisting his figures were right. I decided to cross check my entries with the weighbridge ledger and soon spotted a twenty ton and two six ton loads missing from the weigh book.

"Oh wait a minute," said the weigh clerk. "I was on the 'phone, when Mr. Leech, car thirty, and Flemings weighed out. Now who was I ringing?" and he starts flicking through the 'phone book. "Ah, now I remember — McDonagh, Galway." — and there over McDonagh's name in the 'phone book was the famous thirty-two tons. Good at sums?!

I never had another worry about sums. The daily checking, and totting up the long columns gave me such experience that I never needed an adding machine.

Beyond the Loopline at Butt Bridge is another world, another Dublin. The dockers are a wonderful community of men, and the bellmen, bellwomen, coal hucksters and shop owners were a great family of people to work with. There was very little central heating in those days, and coal was life, power, and bread to nearly all Dublin. The pyramids of coal that ran down Guinness's yard, from Heuston Bridge to the Bloody Bridge at Watling Street had to be seen to be believed. Every major industry and hospital had a stock pile, as well as the daily load of coal. Spencer Dock coal yard ran the length of Guild Street and every square foot of it was covered with mountains of coal.

As the weeks, months and years flew by I knew the coal business inside out and loved every second of it. I rose in rank from posting dockets to weigh clerk on the old beam-type weighbridge, and on to cashier, wages office, accounts office, and depot manager. Now I was interviewing the new clerks and asking, "Are you good at sums?" Thirteen years had passed since my interview and my discovery of Edward Smyth's river masks.

The day the majority of the office workers joined the Union — and went on to form Number One branch of the I.T.G.W.U. as a separate union for coal clerical workers — I went up to Larkin's grave at Glasnevin Cemetery, saluted, prayed and said, "Well, Jem Larkin, what do you think of the white collar workers today, travelling in your footsteps?"

11

Coal Porters and Bellmen

THE FIRST TIME THAT I saw the read for a coal boat it reminded me of the Christmas charity shows in the Rialto Cinema when I was a chisseler. Santa Claus used to stand in the middle of the cinema with a hundred or more children around him, with arms waving and mouths shouting: "Me, Santa." "Here Santa, me Santa." "Give us the sweets Santa." I never remember Santa having enough sweets to go around every child. The faces of those that got them were full of joy and laughter, but the faces of the others who got none were faces of sadness and despair.

The stevedore stood with his back to the coal yard wall on Sir John Rogerson's Quay as he picked the read for a coal boat. The dockers swarmed around him with arms waving and mouths shouting: "Here, me Joe." "Ah Joe, can yeh not see me Joe." "Here, Joe." "How about us Joe?" When the read was over it was shovels in the shed, cards in the cap, and the faces of those who were picked were full of joy and laughter. The faces of the sixty or more who were not picked were full of sadness, despair, and bitterness.

"Did yeh see who he picked — them that couldn't pull the skin off a rice puddin', and good workers like us passed over."

"Are yis going to the Labour?"

"Are there any more boats due up the river to-day?"

While the unemployed grumbled and organised how to

spend the rest of their idle day, the employed were busy testing their Number Seven shovels on the cobblestones. The shovels were heart-shaped and weighed nearly two stone. As well as the diggers picked for the coal boat, a "hooker-on" and a "singer-out" were picked as well. When the coal boat was securely tied to the river wall orders were given by the stevedore: "Man the ship!"

The diggers rushed to the ship's hold to mark their place by Woodbine packets, muffler scarf and cloth caps. The crane driver lifted the iron tubs into the hold and the diggers began filling the tubs. When the tub was filled it was hooked to the crane's jib and the singer-out called out or sang out, "Take it away Charlie." As the tubs filled and the coal fell down in the hold it was nearly impossible to see the diggers for coal dust. The singer-out's bloodshot eyes directed the tubs up and down all day long. The hooker-on stood on the motor lorries, and risked his life everytime a tub of coal swung to him to place on the lorry and undo the crane jib from the tub's hook.

The diggers were on tonnage money and would earn a few pounds on every coal boat, but the hooker-on and singer-out were both on a flat rate of fifteen shillings per boat.

Every few hours the diggers left the boat's hold for what was known as Beero Hour. They all made a bee-line for the nearest public house. Twenty minutes later they were back in the hold stripped to the waist, caps on their heads, some with mufflers around their necks, but all with black coal dust stuck to their sweating bodies.

The reads in those years were held in the street on the quayside. In wintertime, with snow, frost and rain, there were not many spectators. In summertime the visitors from the Isle of Man, Glasgow and Liverpool used to stand watching the read as if it was a football match. The diggers or deep-sea dockers were divided into two groups. The first group were the button-men. The second group were the casual men. The button-men had to be picked first and it was only when there were no more button-men left that the casuals were employed. This caused a certain resentment between the two groups, but I never saw a fight over it. In fact, the resentment was greater between the sons of button-men and the sons of the casual men than it was between their fathers. The button-men's families were on the docks for generations; the casuals were classed as newcomers.

I knew many casuals who walked the docks for years, without getting as much as a month's work. Some of them had given up all hope of work and indulged in the free Loopline porter that spilled on to the lid of the porter barrels at Custom House Quay. It was easy to know the Loopline drinkers, as the red laurel from the barrels was all around their lips and noses. Donnelly's stevedore was Joe Parsons. Joe is dead now, Lord rest him, but he was the finest and fairest stevedore on the Dublin Docks. That was the great thing about the dockers: if you were fair to them they treated you with great respect. If you were unfair to them they threw you into the Liffey. They were tough, hard men, many of them unable to read or write, yet they had a code of ethics among themselves which made them a great body of men to work with.

There was never a dull moment on the Docks. One docker used to join the read, get picked, and then turn around and call his four sons:

"Now lads," he'd say. "There's me spot. Go and dig me fill." Then he'd come over to me in the office and say, "Mr. T, what's the good of havin' childer if they don't work for ya?"

He'd wait outside the office till the four sons did his work. He'd give them a few bob each and then he'd collect his pay.

"Well, like I always say Mr. T, I had to do the same for me ol' fella, and what's the good in havin' childer if they don't work for ya?"

Another docker used to keep me up-to-date on his married daughter living in Parnell Street.

"She's a grand girl, Mr. T, but her and her husband is always fightin'."

And then came the day when the same docker rushes into the office, "Wait till I tell ya Mr. T. Last night, as I was

98

asleep in me bed in Foley Street, didn't I hear banging on the door. I looked out the window and there was me daughter. 'I've left him, Da,' she said. 'I've come home to live with ya.' 'Yeh have in yer arse,' said I. 'Go home, Mary. Yeh made yer bloody bed and now yeh can lie in it!' I wouldn't let her in, Mr. T. No one will point the finger at me, Mr. T. for breaking up a weddin'."

The boats came in daily. The read was held daily and the scene never changed — until one day a casual docker started to cry like a baby because he didn't get a job. The following day his body was fished out of Spencer Dock.

Another casual docker stopped me on my way home one night to tell me that the clergy were going to evict him and his family. He was very upset and took a long time to tell me the full story. It transpired that his next-door neighbour was going to be evicted by the Corporation for non-payment of rent, but that the clergy paid his rent and stopped the eviction. Now he was going to be evicted so he ran to the clergy, but the clergy refused to pay his rent.

"Oh, glory be to God, Mr. T. Who would ever think that the clergy would evict yeh?"

The man in question, the man to be evicted, was a small thin man with very bad eyesight, and he never seemed to be able to get work on the Docks. A few days later he came into the office, smiling. The clergy had a change of heart and paid his rent and he was after getting a fair job as a night watchman.

The night watchman in Donnelly's was Joe Leigh. Joe worked from 6 p.m. at night to 8 a.m. every morning. Joe was a master tailor but due to a slump in the rag trade he had to take up the night watchman's job. He was a member of *Aiseirige* and wore the *Aiseirige* badge in his coat. The dockers were always teasing him because of his *Aiseirige* badge.

"Hey Joe, do you want any dockers for the boat of guns that yeh bring in at night time?" (A few dockers were convinced that Joe was landing boats of guns at Spencer Dock every night.)

"Are yeh really a tailor, Joe?"

"Could yeh make me a suit Joe?"

"Is a tailor a good job Joe?" "Funny there's no work for tailors and there's loads of clothes in the shops."

"It's a cover up, Mr. T. Boats of guns every night while we're sleeping in bed."

Later, when a few dockers saw me speaking on a Sinn Fein platform in Abbey Street, they were fully convinced that Joe and I were bringing in ghost ships loaded with guns every night into Spencer Dock. Every morning from that day onwards, as I walked up Guild Street to open the Spencer Dock coal yard, the coal porters would lift their shovels on their shoulders like soldiers with rifles, and just as I was about to put the key in the lock a few voices would roar out, "Attention!"

The coal yard workers were divided into five sections. The fillers, carters, breasters, drivers and yardmen. The yardmen were paid by the hour, and their job was to break down large slabs of anthracite and grade it into nuts, peas, beans and cobbles by hand. They also worked an old-fashioned, iron, anthracite — crushing machine which made nuts by the dozen and slack by the ton. Anthracite was rationed at the time, and some customers were only allowed six stone a month.

On the first day of every month a titled lady was driven into the coal yard in a black Rolls Royce. The chauffeur got out of the car, changed his cream-coloured driving gloves for a pair of sack-cloth gloves and opened the boot to get out his six-stone container. The lady sat in the car in her pink coat, silver fox fur and black hat, smiling and waving to everyone who passed by the car window.

The coal porters would come to the office window in front of the Rolls Royce and say:

"Will you be needing the car, sir, for the rest of the day?"

"Do you mind if I go home by bike instead of the Rolls?"

"I'm sorry, Mr. T., but I'd nowhere else to park me Rolls." The lady always enjoyed the wit and was most pleasant on every visit.

The fillers who loaded and filled the coal sacks, creel cars

and railway wagons worked in gangs of two men. They were paid on piece-work rates. So it was in their own interest to fill as much tonnage as they could each day. They used a small square-faced shovel that went up and down like lightning. Most of the fillers were big, strong men, with muscles bulging on their arms. They could fill a ten-stone bag of coal in less than ten seconds. The carters and breasters were all small, thin men. To look at them you would never think that they'd be able to lift a ten-stone bag of coal. Not only could they lift the ten-stone bag, they could carry it up six flights of stairs in Mountjoy Square. The carters had their own horse and cart, while the breasters worked on motor lorries. One breaster to every three-ton load of coal. They delivered an average of nine to twelve tons per day which earned them six shillings per three-ton load. The carters on the horse drays delivered one-ton loads about five or six times a day. The carters on the two-ton horse loads delivered between six and eight tons per day. The rate of pay for single tons was three shillings and sixpence, and for two tons, five shillings and eightpence.

There was no sick pay in those days and most of the coal workers suffered 'flu bouts a few times each year. In wet weather the fillers did not work as the coal yard was usually flooded. This meant that the carters and breasters were idle as well. This put all coal workers 'under the hammer', so they had to be paid a fixed rate of £4.00 per week. A carter's and breaster's dream was a fine day, with every load of coal for a coal hole. The Ballast Office coal hole in Westmoreland Street was the favourite pick of every carter. Some of the carters slept with their horses in the stables to be first in line the following morning for the pick of the work.

At eight a.m. every morning after all the cars and carts were weighed in on the weighbridge, and the tare weights recorded, the read of the day's work began —
Six tons for Guinness's
Six tons for Vincent's, The Mater, The Meath, The Rotunda and Patrick Dun's
Six tons for Fry-Cadbury

Six tons for Lemon's
Six tons for Milroy's
Two tons for Ayrton, Saunder's
Two tons for the Ballast Office

One morning the first carter took a long time making up his mind about which load to pick.

"Ah, go wan, Derrie, make up yer mind. Yer holding us all up."

"I don't know," said Derrie, "whether to pick a pint, a bottle of hair oil or a bar of jockolate."

"Ah here give us the two tons for Patrick Dun's and I'll get them to have a look at me bad leg!"

While they were loading the first load I would be preparing the second, third and fourth loads. In the late afternoon the household deliveries would be made. Their day's work, which in some cases started at five a.m., ended about ten p.m. each night. If a customer wasn't at home when they called with the coal, they said they were stubbed. If the customer was at home but gave no tip to the carter, they were called 'rat'.

"That ol' wan, Mr. T., that wanted all the coal at the top of her shed, she was rat, Mr. T., and I nearly broke me back in her shed!"

At one time English coal became scarce and the coal merchants imported Polish coal. Then someone in the head office said that Poland was a Communist country and that the people might object to Polish coal. The problem was solved by calling the coal 'Continental quality'. The carters were instructed to tell the customers it was Continental coal and bring back the customers' reaction.

"Well, Johnny," I said, "what did the customer say when you told her it was Continental coal?"

"Di ya know what she said, Mr. T? She said she didn't give a Continental where it came from, she was frozen waiting for it."

The same carter, Johnny Merrins, overheard me making a date for the Metropole Cinema on the telephone. That night as I was standing in the Metropole queue, trying to impress my new girl-friend, who comes along only Johnny Merrins. He drove his horse and dray along the queue looking for me. I was trying to hold my head down and pretend not to see him.

Then he cried out, "Hey, Mr. T. that ol' wan stubbed me. Don't be givin' out ta me in the mornin'. That ol' wan who you said would be in was out. She stubbed me Mr. T."

He then went on to tell the queue and my new girl-friend about the way I roared at him when he was stubbed.

"He's a terrible man, Miss. Did ya ever hear him roaring?" The queue at this stage were roaring with laughter but I was mortified. To make matters worse Johnny's horse, Hazel, lifted her tail and did a large one beside the queue. Even after Johnny had gone, the brown mountain with steam rising, stood like a monument to the ol' wan that stubbed him.

On the 30th April every year the majority of coal porters were sacked. Only a small skeleton staff was kept to keep the coal yard going during the summer months. The coal porters took up various jobs, selling ice cream, leading donkeys and ponies at the seaside, driving and conducting buses, working on farms in Scotland and England. They all had to be back at the coal yard gate at 8 a.m. on the 1st day of September or else they lost their seniority. I saw two men lose their seniority of thirty-four years by being two days late.

In summertime the coal yard was like a ghost town. In wintertime it was like another world. Hundreds of coal porters, horse carts, motor cars, steam trucks and railway wagons coming and going all day long. The office organised everyone's work and passed the dockets to the yard foreman. My favourite foremen were Pa Caffrey, Joe Smith and Frank Caffrey. They were tough, fair men, whose job it was to get the coal loaded and delivered. Pa Caffrey was an ex-British soldier who was in action at Flanders. He used to tell the story of the night before they went 'over the top'.

"The officer addressed us, Mr. T., he told us that when we got back to Ireland we'd get a pension and a little house in Killester. And when I got back, Mr. T., the Black and Tans were batin' the shite out of me brothers in Gardiner Street."

Joe Smith was the wit. Joe had bad feet and he used to wear boots with the toe-caps cut out of them. When coal was scarce, Joe used to say for a sales policy gimmick "I must tell Maggie to put another two stone in the box."

The day old Mr. McDonagh of Galway gave us two bottles of poteen, Joe drank his bottle and came staggering up to the office.

"Excuse me, Mr. T." he said, "but how many cranes have we in this yard?"

"We've two," I said.

"That's funny," said Joe, "I can see eight!"

McDonagh's were large coal merchants in Galway and their carriers loaded twenty tons of coal every day. The next biggest merchant was Fisher's, Newry, and Leech, Longford. The smallest merchant, or bellman, was Hokey, who loaded one bag of coal on a Granby Row hand cart and sold it by the shovelful around Townsend Street. On a good, cold day, Hokey would sell five bags of coal.

The bellmen were among the hardest workers in the coal trade. Only a few of the elite had motor cars, the vast majority had horses, asses, jinnets, and mules. They sold the coal house-to-house by the stone-weight. Among all the bellmen there was only one bellwoman. She was a fine-looking, fair-haired girl, about twenty-five years of age. She could lift a ten-stone bag of coal off the ground onto her shoulder like any man. That lady bellwoman was always treated with the highest respect by the coal porters and bell-men. The names I remember best were the Farrell Brothers — who are still bellmen today but who have graduated from horses to motor carriers; Mr. Lowndes of Swords, the Maher's, Kennedy's, Ryan's, Mackens, Deveney's and the Royals of Engine Alley. (Da Royal and all his sons were bellmen.) I've often seen twelve Royal's loading coal in George's Quay yard. Da Royal was a great character. I can see him now, standing in his yard in Engine Alley, chopping sticks, logs, or weighing stones of coal, cracking a joke and smiling at everyone. He worked just as hard as every son and grandson.

The coal porters and bellmen of Dublin were the greatest group of people that I ever worked with. They were like show people — they smiled when they were low. The wit of a Dublin coal yard would have to be seen and heard to be fully appreciated. Like the day Hokey got the loan of an ass and cart.

"I won't have to hire a Granby Row hand cart for a shillin', Mr. T. I got a loan of Neddy and the cart for two days."

Hokey loaded four bays of coal on the ass and cart and pulled him onto the weighbridge. When he was weighed-out correctly the ass would not move off the scales. Hokey pushed it, pulled it, lit matches under it, but still the Ass refused to move. The sweat was pouring off Hokey as he came to the office window.

He took off his cap to mop his brow and then he said:

"Mr. T., you're an intelligent man. Could you tell me something, Mr. T.?"

I said to myself quickly, "I hope he doesn't ask me how to get the ass off the scales."

"Mr. T.," said Hokey again, "Can you tell me how in the name of God did Jesus Christ ever escape into Egypt on an ass?"